MW01515638

Looking Over God's Shoulder

Larkin A. Yandell

Copyright 2015
By
Larkin A. Yandell

ISBN 978-1-940609-44-7 Soft cover

All rights reserved
No part of this book may be reproduced or transmitted in
any form or by any means, electronic or mechanical,
including photocopying, recording, or by any information
storage and retrieval system, without permission in writing
from the copyright owner.

Bible verses are from the KJV.

This book was printed in the United States of America.

To order additional copies of this book order from:

www.amazon.com

FWB

FWB Publications

Columbus, Ohio

Table of Contents

FOREWORD

Looking Over God's Shoulder
Powerful moments in a lifetime of ministry

Larkin A. Yandell has been peeking over God's shoulder for a very long time. Just as a small child stretches and strains to see what his father is doing at his workbench, Pastor Yandell has delighted in watching God at work.

Born on December 13, 1927, in Latimer County of southeastern Oklahoma, he was the twelfth and final child of his parents, Joseph Elza ("Elzie") and Effie Yandell. (Unfortunately, only eight of those children lived to adulthood.) Although his father was a well-known pastor/evangelist in that region, Larkin was not born again until he was a member of the United States Navy.

After his brief hitch in the Navy ended, He was ordained as a Free Will Baptist minister at 21 years of age and installed as the part-time pastor of a small church at Norris, a tiny community near Red Oak, Oklahoma.

At this writing, Pastor Yandell has walked with God for nearly 70 years. In those years he has pastored three churches in Oklahoma (in Norris, Tulsa, and Oklahoma City), and three more in California (in the cities of Modesto, Concord, and Visalia).

At 88 years of age, Larkin Yandell is the pastor of the Demaree Road Free Will Baptist Church in Visalia, California where he has served since 1973. These days, he doesn't get around as well as he once did. Macular Degeneration has stolen much of his vision (he is legally blind), but it has done nothing to dampen his faith or desire to see what God is up to.

I know this to be true, of course, because Larkin A. Yandell is my father. I have witnessed his abiding faith in God in good times and bad. In fact, when I was a high school senior I faced a crisis of faith. I had to decide if I truly believed the Christian story or not. After all, jettisoning Christianity would open up a whole new set of behaviors and opportunities for me, or so some of my friends said. But, try as I might, I could not deny that what I saw in my father's life and character was real.

Like the vast majority of pastors, Dad has never led a mega-church of thousands. He's never written a bestseller and never hosted a highly rated television show. Like most small church pastors, he has worn a lot of different hats from time to time: janitor, groundskeeper, secretary, construction worker/supervisor, bus driver, and many more. In all of it, he has faithfully sought to know and do what is in the best interests of the church, often at his own expense.

This book is a compilation of articles my father wrote over a period of several years. They first appeared in the Demaree Church's newsletter and they describe incidents that occurred at various periods of his pastoral ministry. Some are chronicles of triumphant works of God. A couple record tragic events rooted in the unbelief of man. All of them, however, provide readers with profound, potentially life-changing record of God at work in our world.

The events described in these pages took place during several decades. As such, the terms used are consistent with the era in which they occurred. There has been no attempt to edit for political correctness or contemporary sensibilities. Some names have been changed in respect for the individuals involved. In addition, readers will notice that biblical quotations are from the King James Version, Dad's preferred translation.

In these pages you will find accounts of God's work in the lives of people Dad has encountered along the way. Some will amaze you, others will inspire you, and one or two may even break your heart. These are the words of a humble man who aspires to walk with the limitless, all-powerful God one day at a time and share with the rest of us what he has seen God do. May these words inspire us to do the same.

Jonathan Yandell
Editor

Larkin and Wilmatine Yandell

Chapter 1

~

CHRISTY IS MISSING

I was still working on the last bite of my late lunch when I heard a car sliding to a stop in front of the parsonage. I reached the door in time to see a cloud of dust billowing up from our gravel parking lot and a woman racing toward our front porch in what appeared to me to be an advanced state of hysteria. She was yelling, but I could not understand a word she was saying.

We met at the top of the steps. I took her by the shoulders-holding her until she quieted down. When she gained control of her emotions I released my grip. She struggled to speak, but finally blurted out the words: "Christy is missing!"

I was taken aback. Did I know someone named Christy? No one came to mind.

"Who is Christy?" I said, "And who are you?"

"I am Mary," she said, with desperation still in her voice. "I live on the east side of Tulsa. Christy is a little girl living at the end of the new road the county has opened up. She is a little past three years of age."

"I was on that road," she continued, "looking for property that my husband and me might be able to buy, when I saw the woman racing toward me waving her arms for me to stop. I could see she was crying, so I stopped. She told me her little girl, Christy, was missing. She asked me if I would please go for help. I remembered passing this church on my way to look for property and it was the only place I could think of to go for help. On my way here, I panicked."

I asked if authorities had been notified. Mary didn't know. Could she lead me to where she met the lady who told her the little girl was missing? She said she could.

I followed her in my car, thinking as we went that there was nothing in my past that prepared me for search and rescue. Or was there? Down the halls of my memory I could hear echoes of my parents cautioning me about the dangers of snakes, stock ponds, rushing streams, and low clouds covering the mountaintops. Would these be a starting place to look for Christy? Perhaps.

I had traveled the road we were on. Just a few months back I was on this road, doing community visitation. I had even stopped at some of the houses. But I could not recall seeing a pond or swimming pool. No rushing streams or snakes, either. And, today, I could see there were no low clouds covering the hilltops. However, I knew there were hundreds of acres of unfriendly scrub oaks, briars, tall grass, and wild animals.

As we drove, I was surprised at how fast the area was building up. Several families had purchased five-acre tracts, built homes, and were in the process of landscaping their yards.

Mary's brake lights came on. I braked, straining to see why she was stopping. Then I noticed the house, almost completely hidden by trees. This must be the place-the end of the road. As I parked, I saw a huge pile of reddish dirt. A shudder ran through my body when I realized this family had dug a pond or swimming pool.

I feared the worst as I hurried toward the pile of dirt. A lady came rushing toward me identifying herself as Christy's mother. Without slackening my pace I asked what was behind the massive pile of dirt.

"A pond," she replied.

I broke into a run, only to be stopped in my tracks when she called out, "There is no water in the pond! We finished it last week and it hasn't rained since we dug it," she explained.

Approaching cars halted our conversation with her husband's vehicle leading the way. Workers from the plant where he was employed followed him. The whole plant had shut down. Business as usual could wait. Christy was missing and finding her was the priority. Only one person remained at the plant to answer the phones. Strangers calling the plant on business were told of the crisis. Soon even some of them arrived to join in the search.

The employees of the plant weren't the only ones who were coming. Sirens could be heard in the distance and momentarily sheriff's cars began arriving, followed by an ambulance and medical team. Trucks and trailers carrying horses were next. Finally, a real search and rescue team came, trained and equipped to comb the hundreds of acres for Christy who had now been missing for more than three hours.

A massive search and rescue was about to be launched. A helicopter, equipped with powerful searchlights, was ordered to stand by as plans were made to search through the night, if necessary.

Professionals, trained in search and rescue for just such an occasion, led the effort. Almost a hundred people like me, untrained but willing to help, formed a line with only a few feet between us. We walked through the underbrush as best we could, calling Christy's name, waiting momentarily for her to respond, and then repeating the call again and again. "Christy! Christy!" The little girl's name rang out across the field, even when most of those calling her could not be seen for the brush.

Finally, the word came, Christy had been found! She was approximately four miles from home. Somehow she had made it through the brush-choked field and found her way to a small clearing at the top of a hill. It was there that a mounted member of the search and rescue team found her.

The search was over just a little before dark. It ended with the joyous return of a little girl who was bruised, scratched, and very, very tired. So tired, in fact, she went to sleep even while people were talking and celebrating her rescue.

Driving home that evening I thought of the effort that had been made to find Christy. For the sake of a missing little girl, people left families, jobs, and businesses. They paid whatever cost was necessary to find her. It was the most Christlike thing most of the rescuers had ever done.

Just a reminder...

Lord, thank You for seeking us when we wandered far from You. Thank You most of all for finding us and bringing us back home. Please help us to join in Your loving pursuit of others that are lost. Amen.

Chapter 2

CAROL IS SLEEPING . . . THREE YEARS AND COUNTING

Charles finished his work shift at 3:00 p.m. His weekend was beginning in the middle of my week. The time off would give Charles a day when he could visit his cousin in another city. He stopped by the parsonage on his way home and invited me to go with him. He wanted me to meet his aunt-a woman he described as the most courageous mother he had ever known.

Our visit would be timed to coincide with his cousin's nineteenth birthday. There would not be a birthday cake or party. In fact, his cousin would not respond in any way; nor could she, as far as anyone knew. She had suffered a serious head injury in a car accident three years earlier. The injury had left her comatose.

On the day of our visit, the drive to the home of Charles' aunt gave him less than an hour to prepare his inexperienced 24 year-old pastor for the visit. Try as he might, he could not find the words or the way to explain what I was about to see. Finally, he simply said I would just have to experience it for myself.

It was mid-spring in Oklahoma. A gentle breeze teased the leaves and blooming flowers into a swaying victory dance. Creation was celebrating new life after a long, hard winter. It seemed appropriate. We had come to celebrate a life that was once vibrant and vivacious, filled with laughter and play-the dance of youth. But now, that young life was strangely silent and still-waiting for a new life and a victory dance of another sort. This was a heart held in the loving hands of God. Only He could and did understand.

In silence, I prayed, giving thanks to God for my health, my youth, and His grace. My prayer ended when Charles slowed the car and pulled over to the curb, stopping in front of his aunt's home.

"Auntie is waiting and watching for us," Charles said with a chuckle as we got out of the car. I turned to see an attractive, motherly woman in her forties coming down the steps to meet us. Charles met her halfway between the car and the porch. They greeted each other warmly. Both had clearly been looking forward to our visit.

"Charles," I heard her say, "I was expecting you to come, even before you called." Turning to me, she explained, "He always comes on Carol's birthday."

Charles introduced me as his pastor and his aunt made me feel as though I was one of the family. I could tell she was the kind of person who always had room for one more in the family circle. "Let's go inside," she suggested, leading the way into the house. "I know you are eager to see Carol."

We entered a spacious, but homey, living room. I glanced around. Everything was in its place and it all seemed to say welcome. Immediately, I felt at home.

Pausing inside, Charles' aunt asked if I knew about Carol. "A little," Charles answered. She led us into Carol's room and announced our presence.

"Carol, we have company," she said. "Charles and his pastor have come to see us and help us celebrate your birthday."

Charles greeted Carol and introduced me as his pastor. I spoke to her even though I felt a little awkward. Charles continued talking to Carol.

"Carol, you are just as beautiful as ever. I can hardly believe you are 19 today. It seems like only yesterday that you and I were playing baseball together. That was before I went away to war. You couldn't have been over seven years old, and look at you today. You are now a beautiful young woman of 19!"

Charles and his aunt continued visiting, including Carol in their conversation. I looked, listened, and learned. It was hard for me to fully grasp the moment. Before me was a beautiful young woman who was unconscious, and had been for three years. Yet, her hair and face was picture perfect. She lay sleeping on a three-quarter bed, with a stylish hairdo and fresh makeup on her face. She looked as though she was just resting after a morning trip to the beauty salon.

Our visit lasted about an hour. We told Carol goodbye and walked to the front porch. Charles' aunt asked if she could tell me about Carol and the night that changed her life. We sat down.

"Pastor," she began, "you may think us strange the way we talked to Carol. Her doctors have told us that, though she is in a coma, she may be able to hear some-if not all-of what is being said in her presence. The doctors cautioned us not to speak negatively or falsely about her condition or any prospect she may have of waking up.

They are fine Christians and have told us she is in the hands of God. Should God wake her up, all praise and honor goes to Him. If she doesn't wake up, in time, her body will shut down and she will move to Heaven. We are here to care for Carol as though she will wake up at any moment."

"I am a trained beautician," she continued. "I had my own shop at the time Carol was injured. When we brought her home I sold my shop so I could stay with her and care for her. I believe God directed me to Beauty College, and I was especially trained to take care of my daughter. I count it a blessed privilege to care for her. Every morning I fix her hair and her face . . . I call it my 'mothering ministry.' I believe it is most pleasing to God. I abound with energy and have never felt the need of being relieved or the need of a vacation. I want to be here when, and if, Carol awakes. I keep my mind stayed on God, and I have peace from Him. Isaiah 26:3 has become real to me."

She shifted positions, and the tone of her voice changed slightly as her eyes lit up with excitement. "Carol was saved at the age of 13, and she has been a very strong witness since her conversion. Christ was her life, and she wanted everyone to know Him, especially the kids she went to school with."

It was about 5:00 p.m. on the night that changed their lives when a group of kids from their church had driven to Oklahoma City for a youth rally. It was Carol's birthday. She was 16 years old. Their plans included stopping at a favorite spot after the rally for ice cream in celebration of her birthday. They would be a little late getting home.

On their way for ice cream, it happened. A young man, intoxicated from a different kind of party, was driving at high speed on a newly opened divided highway. He was on his way to get more drinks for the party when he lost control of his car. The car ran off the pavement, through the center median, and crashed head-on into the vehicle in which Carol was a passenger. The driver was killed. Other kids in the car with Carol suffered minor injuries, but she was seriously hurt.

Charles' aunt paused. Her eyes filled with tears. "Pastor that poor mother of the boy that was killed" she said. "My heart and prayers are still for her. I attended the graveside funeral with his mother and I'll never forget her words. 'I will never see him again. He died lost. Now he is forever lost. There will never be another party for him.'"

"Pastor, I thank God for my Carol . . . and I believe her witness for Him has been more effective these last three years than in the first three years of her Christian life. She is a silent reflector of the Light of the world. And that light, Jesus Christ, is shining into the sin-darkened hearts of people almost weekly. At first it was a stream of young people coming to see her every week. Then it slowed to just a trickle. Now, not as many, but some still come at various times. All of them know of Carol becoming a Christian before the accident and that God is now using her as a silent witness. I cannot explain it, but as they see her lying peacefully, waiting for God's wake up call, they are impressed with the urgent need of receiving Christ while they are yet conscious lest something like the accident should happen to them."

With that, she seemed to end her testimony. I felt I should comment in some way and said the only thing that came to mind. "It must be a great comfort to you to know Carol was saved before the accident and that God is using her as a silent missionary to witness to others." She nodded. "You are a most remarkable woman and mother," I added. "I can sense God's presence in you even as we talk."

"That's my desire," she said with a smile.

Our visit ended with all three of us praying together. Charles and I returned to Tulsa and I was left alone with my thoughts. Deeply moved, I sensed the Holy Spirit teaching me truths I would need and use in ministering to others.

Of the things I learned, I think foremost was the urgency of having a saving relationship with God while we are capable of hearing and responding to the gospel of Christ. No one is exempted from the accidents or disease that may render us incapable of ever responding to God's grace through faith in Jesus Christ (Ephesians 2:8-9). The decision to be a Christ-follower is too important to be postponed.

Buoyed by her own relationship with God and the assurance of her daughter's, Carol's mother was not bitter. She did not blame God for the horrible accident that left her daughter in a coma. Instead, she worked on her relationship with God and gave thanks to Him for living in her-for He alone knew the depth of both of their pain . . . and yours.

Lord, we confess that we often do not understand what You are doing, but that doesn't change the fact that You have a plan and it is being carried out in perfect detail. Help us to trust Your wisdom and lift You up in every circumstance of life . . . like Carol and her mother. Amen.

Chapter 3

IN JESUS' NAME

Our youngest son was about to be born. In addition to insurance coverage, I needed $300 for the doctor. I kept up with the pre-natal expenses, but I didn't have the rest of the money, so I turned to my heavenly Father for help. I prayed in Jesus' name, but I must confess it was without understanding, and somewhat a mystery to me that I would expect help from God through such a prayer.

I knew in my heart that Jesus had given the disciples more than a mere formula or spiritual technique to get things from God when He said, "Whatsoever ye shall ask the Father in My name, He may give it ye (John 15:16b). But I did not know that what I was about to experience in a real-life situation would result in a better understanding of asking in Jesus' name.

Delivery time for the baby's arrival drew near. The doctor's secretary called to remind me of the $300 I owed and wanted to know how I would handle it. I responded, "I'll pay it in lump sum before or the day after the birth."

After hanging up the phone, I wondered why I had made such a promise. I had no idea where to get the money. I worried the rest of the day and into the night. I finally dropped off to sleep, only to awaken suddenly. "Man," the name of my brother-in-law, came to mind (His given name was actually Cornelius McCann, but when he was young his family called him Little Man. However, when that Choctaw Indian boy grew into a man that was taller and stronger than anyone around, the "Little" was dropped.) Why would I think of him? He lived 185 miles from me. Had something happened to him or the family?

In my imagination, I could see all sorts of bad things happening to them. I prayed for the family. I found no peace and never went back to bed. Toward morning, I made coffee and did my devotional readings. I was finishing Philippians 4 when God comforted my heart with verse 19: ". . . but my God shall supply all your need according to His riches in glory by Christ Jesus." (I wrote in the margin, "That which He doesn't supply, I don't need.")

I drifted off into a period of half-asleep thought, but was startled awake by the sound of the paperboy tossing the newspaper on the porch. The cool fall breeze felt good when I stepped out onto the porch to get the paper. I paused in the breeze, thinking about my brother-in-law and his family. I decided I would go to see about them. The fear of bad things happening to them was gone, but there was a sense of urgency driving me to see them.

I left soon after breakfast for the four-hour drive to Red Oak, Oklahoma. As I drove along, my mind went back to the promise I had made to the doctor. I still did not know where I would get the $300 I had promised to the doctor, but I was not panicky like I was the night before. Instead, I was very calm, a fact that caused me to wonder if God had already answered my prayer. I felt a surge of excitement just thinking about the possibility. *Why not?* I reasoned. *After all, I did ask in Jesus' name.*

Traffic thickened and I concentrated on my driving. It was a beautiful autumn drive and the trees were wearing their fall colors proudly. I gave thanks to God for the roadside beauty as He prepared them for their winter rest.

Nearing Red Oak, I thought of my reason for being there. I would drive the remaining eight miles to my brother-in-law's place, check on them, and eat lunch with them. (My sister, Willie Bee, always had good things to eat.) Then I would start back to Oklahoma City.

Man and Bee were surprised to see me. "What a coincidence," they said. "We were just talking about you this morning. Is everything alright? Is the baby here?"

There was a sudden urge to ask them for a loan of $300. I couldn't believe I would even think of such a thing. There is no way my brother-in-law would loan me money, even if he had it . . . which he didn't. I remembered a time when I asked him to loan me his squirrel dog (a dog specifically trained for hunting red fox squirrels). He refused, saying I would ruin his dog. So, I stood before them in awkward silence.

"I know something is wrong," my sister said. "What is it?"

"I told them the whole story. My brother-in-law turned his head and spit through his teeth at a bee that was visiting a fall flower. Turning back, he fumbled with his wallet, pulled out a blank check, and handed it to me. I stared at the unsigned check, wondering if he was playing a cruel joke on me.

Noticing the confused look on my face, my

brother-in-law began to explain his plan. He said he would loan me the amount I needed for the doctor, but there was always a chance for complications and I would need more than $300. The blank unsigned check was to meet my need. He added, "You fill the check out for the amount you need and sign my name to the check. Then write your name underneath mine." He said the bank would honor the check when it came through. I thanked him and my sister for the help. We visited a short while before I left for Oklahoma City.

On my way home, I gave thanks to God for answered prayer. While thinking about the actions of my brother-in-law, I realized his goodness to me and the trust he had placed in me. With one blank unsigned check, he had trusted me with his entire bank account, whatever amount it might be. He trusted me to take only what I asked for and a bit more if complications drove up the doctor's charges. He trusted me not to abuse his trust in me. I even thought, *why would he be so generous to me?* It was because I was a member of the family. Family members have rights and privileges others do not.

The baby was born and I went the next day to pay the doctor. There were no additional fees, so I made the check for the $300 I owed. I signed my brother-in-law's name: *Cornelius McCann by L. A. Yandell.* I was nervous when I handed the check to the office girl. She looked at the check, noting that it was an out of town bank and that I had signed a name other than my own. "What is this?" she asked. I explained. "I am asking in my brother-in-law's name for $300. He has the money and told me to ask for it in his name and the bank would honor it." She shook her head saying, "I'll try it. If it doesn't work, we will be contacting you."

I left the doctor's office with a good feeling, not just

because my bill was paid, but I felt like I had a better understanding of what it meant to ask in Jesus' name.

Jesus, speaking of His death, comforted His disciples with these words, "And in that day ye shall ask me nothing. Verily, verily, I say unto you, whatsoever ye shall ask the Father in my name, He will give it you. Hitherto have ye ask nothing in My name. ask, and ye shall receive, that your joy may be full" (John 16:23).

The insight I received from my brother-in-law's experience helped me to understand a deeper truth in this way. He had riches I knew nothing about in the local bank. I was a family member in need. Because of my relationship, I could ask the bank for money in my brother-in-law's name and receive it.   So it is in my spiritual family. My heavenly Father has riches I know nothing about. As a member of the family, I can ask Him for my needs and He will supply them according to His riches in glory through Jesus Christ my Savior/Lord (Philippians 4:19).

Are you a member of God's family? If so, you can ask the Father for your needs in the name of Jesus.

Thank You, Father, that Your resources are never exhausted and You delight in giving good gifts to Your children! Grant us grace to trust You to meet all our needs when we ask in Jesus' name. Amen.

Chapter 4

THE BAG LADY IS MY SISTER

"Be not forgetful to entertain strangers: for thereby some have entertained angels unawares" (Hebrews 13:2).

She was crossing SE 15th Street in Oklahoma City. It wasn't my first time to see her. She was a common sight on South Robinson, a light industrial section of the city. The area was mostly run down rentals in those days, but there was a small park and a few well-kept homes. As always, she was pulling her red wagon and looking for treasures she could collect.

Today was different from other times when I had seen her. She was only a few city blocks from our church, coming from an area called "the flats" ("up towners" called it the slum). Her Western Flyer wagon was filled—piled high above the small sideboards—with treasures she had picked up off the streets and out of garbage cans.

I continued slowing my car and finally brought it to a complete stop as she struggled to keep her cargo from tumbling into the street. She made it to the curb, but when she lifted the front of the wagon to the top of the curb, her treasures suddenly tumbled off into the street.

Help her!

Who? Me? Why should I?

I eased my car over to the curb and parked—still wondering about the thoughts that came rushing into my mind. Finally, I exited the car and went back to help.

She was bent over at the waist—legs straight as a fence post—picking up her lost treasures.

"Good afternoon. May I help you?" I asked.

Without straightening up, she turned her head to see who was speaking. When she smiled I saw one lonely yellowish tooth. Her skin was dark and wrinkled from overexposure to the Oklahoma weather, but it complemented her twinkling blue eyes.

Her eyes that told me I could help as she continued to retrieve her treasures. Together, we loaded her wagon with the fallen items. She never straightened up until the job was done.

When she stretched to her full height she was still a small woman—well under five feet tall. For the first time she looked me over. Her gaze passed from my carefully groomed hair, to my blue suit, down to my shined shoes. I waited for her comment, wondering if I would pass her inspection.

"You must be a preacher," she said. "Only a preacher would wear clothes like yours on a hot day like this."

I smiled, slightly amused by her observation. My thoughts whirled.

How would she know about preachers? She's a "bag lady!" Why don't I just wish her a good day and get on with my church visitation? Or, could talking to this bag lady actually be part of my church visitation?

A verse of Scripture came to mind: "Pure religion and undefiled before God and the Father is this, to visit the fatherless and widows in their affliction, and keep himself unspotted from the world" (James 1:27). Now I was even more confused.

What is God trying to tell me? Or, is He trying to tell me anything? Is this bag lady a widow? Is she fatherless? Did she grow up as an orphan? How would Christ respond to this little woman who scoured the streets and garbage cans for her livelihood?

I introduced myself and handed her one of my business cards. She looked the card over and reached for a string tied around her neck. As she tugged at the string she remarked, "I've got another card. One from the sheriff." When she pulled the string free from her clothing I was surprised to see a small sack dangling at the end of it. She carefully removed two safety pins and pulled out the other card. It really was a personalized card from the county sheriff.

"The sheriff told me to call him if I ever needed him," she commented. "He said anytime day or night was okay."

I watched her place my card with the sheriff's card as she turned away from me. She pulled her blouse out at the neck, dropping the little sack down inside her clothing. This little bag lady was intriguing. I had to know more about her. In a strange sort of way I even felt a sense of kindred. *Is she a Christian?* I wondered.

"I would like to be friends with you," I said, "I pastor the Central Avenue Church, which is only about three or four blocks from where we are. It's the red brick building with the lighted church sign out front."

The bag lady seemed to be smiling as she drifted down memory lane. Not knowing what she was thinking, I waited for her response.

"I went to a red brick church one time. They had donuts and soup sometime." She paused momentarily, then continued. "They moved away. I don't know where. Then another church came. I went one time—no one would talk to me. I didn't go back. They moved away and someone tore the church down. Now there is no church."

"What is your name?" I inquired.

"Taylor," she replied.

I sensed a budding friendship. We were warming up to each other and talking was becoming easier for both of us.

"Do you go to church now?" I asked.

"No," she replied.

"Would you like to come to our church? We would love to have you, and we will come and get you if you need transportation."

"Yes, if I can bring my wagon. I will walk."

I recalled the words of Jesus when He came to his disciples walking upon a stormy sea, "It is I; be not afraid" (John 6:20). *Is Jesus saying to me that He is dwelling in this bag lady and I am not to be afraid?* A warm feeling washed over me. *Is this bag lady actually my sister in Christ?*

"Sure," I answered, "you may bring your wagon. I will be looking forward to seeing you soon."

With that I continued on my way, visiting others. But I could not keep the bag lady out of my mind. *Will she really come to church? Where will she park her wagon? Will she bring it inside the church—perhaps down the aisle? Will she park it in someone's favorite parking space? What's the rest of her name? Where is her family—if she has one?* One thing was certain; she was mysterious.

As the weeks passed I continued thinking about my encounter with the bag lady . . . and her, shall we say, *odorous* body. The smell that surrounded her seemed to be a mixture of sweat, armpits, and . . . well, other aromas. It made me wonder if this scent was unique to bag ladies and other people who slept on the streets, in alleys, parks, or under bridges. I smiled to myself thinking about her odor mingling with that of the colognes and perfumes worn by the people that attended our church. Nevertheless I was getting excited just imagining the difference she would make in our Sunday evening service . . . if she came.

A few days later, the people were coming in for the Sunday evening service. The parking lot was filling up, but the bag lady had not arrived. I was greeting people when I noticed our song leader and pianist making their way to the front of the church. Glancing at my watch, it was still five minutes until starting time.

I was moving toward the front when I sensed that others were coming in. Turning toward the back doors, I saw Mrs. Taylor, without her wagon, making her way down the center aisle. (I later learned she had parked her wagon outside.) The ushers had already greeted her warmly and now stood watching her slowly walk down the aisle. I went to meet her. Not knowing how to introduce her to others, I greeted her warmly and asked if she were Miss or Mrs. Taylor.

"My husband left when my Jimmy was born," she replied. "I don't know where he is and I don't care. I hope I never see him again."

I asked where she would like to sit. She chose the second row from the front—where Mrs. Peters always sat. Sister Peters was a sweet elderly lady, a full-sized woman, with a humble spirit and a heart full of love. She gladly turned a bit to allow Mrs. Taylor to take a seat.

Mrs. Taylor squeezed by Sister Peters and continued standing, gazing at the baptistery.

"That's a pretty picture on the back wall of the baptistery, isn't it?" I remarked.

"I was dunked one time," she commented, her eyes still fixed on the baptistery.

I had my answer. I would introduce her as my sister in the Lord and discover the details of her spiritual life later.

I walked to the pulpit to begin the service. The song leader was in his place, grinning so big his eyes were just slits. The pianist, leaning slightly to the left to look around the piano light, gave me a large smile. I turned to face the audience. The ushers, standing at their place at the entrance of the room, were smiling too. Even the congregation seemed unusually happy, with only a few exceptions. The ones who weren't smiling had their eyes fixed on the bag lady.

Ignoring the frowns, I greeted the congregation enthusiastically. "Tonight we have a very special blessing. I am privileged and honored to introduce to you my new friend and sister in the Lord. Please welcome Sister Taylor!"

The bag lady's eyes lit up. She stood, waving a wrinkled handkerchief at the people. She turned her head from side to side; she flashed the same smile I'd first seen on the street, exposing that same lonely yellowish tooth for all to see. Instantly, Sister Taylor won the hearts of that Sunday night congregation.

We stood and prayed, then I went to my chair and the singing began. I looked at the hymnal, but my heart wasn't singing. Somehow I sensed something different about the bag lady. What was it? My thoughts drifted back to the moment I greeted her in the center aisle. I had shaken her hand and placed my left hand on her shoulder as I directed her to the pews. What's missing? Then it hit me. The scent! I had not ever noticed the odor that was once so offensive to my super-sensitive nose.

I immediately joined the congregation in singing, *The Old Time Religion*. When we got to the second verse, we sang of how the old time religion "Makes me love everybody." I knew then why I hadn't noticed the odor.

After the service, I waited my turn to talk with Sister Taylor. In our short conversation I discovered that her "Jimmy" was now a grown man, living with a family of his own in Stockton, California. He stayed in touch with his mother, as best he could, encouraging her to call him collect, since she could neither read nor write. But she never did.

On more than just a few occasions, Jimmy would contact the office of the county sheriff asking them to find his mother. The sheriff took the first call personally. That explained why she had his personalized business card. At other times, it was a deputy that would check on her.

There were other questions I wanted to ask, but Sister Taylor had to leave. I watched as she pulled her red wagon down the sidewalk toward SE 15th Street. I saw two large red reflectors on the back of her wagon and felt a little better about her safety as she walked in the dark. One question did concern me—where will she sleep tonight? I thought about following her, but then it occurred to me that even a bag lady wouldn't want to be stalked, no matter what the reason.

I watched as she disappeared into the darkness, then I walked the half-block to my home. A Sunday night snack, the recliner, and even the late newscast, did little to divert my thoughts from Sister Taylor. Mentally, I could not release her until I prayed for her and made plans to locate her on Monday morning.

Monday morning, I drove to the area where I thought another red brick church once stood. I arrived in the area a little past 8:00 a.m. The neighborhood was undergoing some great change. Many buildings were completely demolished, making way for a new freeway bypass and the accompanying new commercial business that would cater to travelers.

Led by the Holy Spirit, I believe, I stopped at one well-kept house. An elderly couple greeted me at the door and with a warm welcome invited me in for coffee. Being eager for conversation about the area, I accepted.

This dear couple was eager for a visit as well, and they enjoyed talking about their home. All of their eight children grew up and attended school in that area. (The old school was now being used for some kind of social work.) They had bought the lot on which they built their house when the area first opened for development. They had lived in their dream home for years and had no intention to leave it. They planned to just leave for Heaven from that very spot, just as soon as the Good Lord said it was time for them to go.

The old couple told me about the red brick church. They were once members of that congregation. They called it "The Old-time Methodist." They even had fond memories of a social time with donuts before the Sunday service and unforgettable soup suppers on Wednesday night.

They voted against the church relocating to the northwest part of Oklahoma City. When the move was made anyway, they could no longer attend, so they began going to Capitol Hill Baptist, just across the river, with friends who gave them a ride.

By now my heart was beating faster with excitement and my throat was dry. I had to ask about Sister Taylor. Did they know her, and if so, what did they know? Smiling at each other, they began their story about their acquaintance with Sister Taylor.

"Now that lady was some lady!" he said. "She had been on the streets for many years. People that tried to talk with her found her hard to understand. Her talk was more like mumbling and made little sense. She had Indian blood in her veins."

"Tell him about her coming to church," his wife interjected.

"Well," he began, "that was something else. It was on a Mother's Day when in walked this bag lady with a fine young couple from California. The funny thing was that no one recognized her in a new dress with her hair all done up nice. She even wore a corsage of three red roses. The young man introduced her as his mother, saying, 'We are the Taylor's.' She continued coming once in a while, as long as the church was there. She only came on a Sunday morning or a Wednesday night—I guess it was when she was short on food. We still see her on the streets. That's about all I can tell you."

I thanked them for their hospitality and good coffee, and started my drive back toward the church. My new friends had told me much about Sister Taylor and, perhaps unknown to them, had confirmed the things she had told me. Still, I was eager to discover more details of her life—especially her spiritual life.

On my way back to the church, I spotted Sister Taylor's red wagon at the side of a popular workingman's restaurant. This place only served breakfast and lunch. They specialized in homemade yeast rolls—all you could eat with butter, honey, or jelly. They always kept the hot bread on your table until you finished your meal, whether it was breakfast or lunch . . . my kind of place.

I had a thought. *Maybe I could buy Sister Taylor lunch.* I pulled into the parking lot and made my way to the restaurant entrance. Stepping inside, I looked for Sister Taylor. Someone called out to me, "Sit wherever you like!" I chose a table facing the front door, with a view into the kitchen area and back door.

To my surprise, when the backdoor opened I saw Sister Taylor headed outside. At that very moment, the waitress brought hot rolls to my table. I ordered a plate lunch, a popular vegetable plate, and excused myself, telling the waitress that I would be right back.

Rushing outside, I saw Sister Taylor pulling her wagon across the parking lot. I called to her. She was surprised to see me, and even more surprised when I invited her to lunch. She refused the invitation, however, explaining that she had already had lunch. She said she ate with the man and woman who owned the restaurant. I would learn later that she often ate with them in what they called their "private dining room"—a section of the kitchen with a table and chairs for four.

I returned to my lunch, enjoying it a bit more knowing that Sister Taylor also had a good lunch. I was excited at the prospect of having a bag lady call me, "Pastor." It would be the first, and perhaps only, time I would be a pastor to a bag lady.

I remembered the words Jesus spoke, "For ye have the poor always with you" (Matthew 26:11a). Why would I think of these words at this particular time? What are His plans for me? Are there other bag ladies or homeless people that I will pastor? I wondered about the spiritual life of other people in similar circumstances. How many are my sisters and brothers in Christ? Do they have pastors? Is there a caring church to love and lead them?

One thing God seemed to settle in my mind—they are not all addicts. Some homeless people have found, for various reasons, their niche in society. In the days ahead, God would teach me, as a pastor to a bag lady, that I must respect her as a person and love and minister to her as He would, for I am His ambassador (2 Corinthians 5:20).

My pastoral relationship to Sister Taylor might be described as "different." There were no home visits, discipleship studies, or socializing. No spoken expressions of endearment—just acts of kindness and warm greetings, genuine respect for each other, and Christian love—a relationship that demanded no payback from each other. Refreshing!

As time passed, my relationship to Sister Taylor was producing change in me. I came to the place where I actually had a great admiration for her. She faced every day with a simple trust in God—trusting Him for daily bread. She would do her part—scouring the garbage cans and streets, and God would do His part. She would graciously accept gifts of food, money, and clothes from various sources as His provision for her needs. Just as God can change a sinner into a saint, He can also change trash into treasures. I saw it, not on one occasion, but many.

I never heard Sister Taylor complain about her lot in life. She lived it without blaming others. She was comfortable in who she was and in what she did. I never tried to move her from her comfort zone, believing it would have been a disaster for her. Instead, I prayed for wisdom to enter her world, not as one superior to the other, but as equals in the eyes of God.

I wanted to show a genuine interest in what she was interested in, and to show appreciation for her skills and accomplishments. I wanted to exchange encouragements with her. I wanted to be a pastor and friend to her. To do this, I would have to deal with ingrained concepts and prejudice toward certain classes of people.

Weeks turned into months. The amount of time escapes me, but I knew my pastoral duties at that church were coming to an end. One day, the ringing of my office phone interrupted my thoughts.

The caller, a woman, inquired, "Are you Pastor Yandell and do you know a Ms. Taylor?" I answered yes. She introduced herself saying, "I'm the lead nurse on the east wing of the first floor of the County Hospital. Ms. Taylor was hit by a car last Friday evening and was brought to the hospital with bruises and a bump on the head. She apparently received no serious injuries, but we kept her through the weekend for observation. Pastor, we would like for you to come for a visit with her and to evaluate her condition. After you have completed your visit, we want to meet with you for your evaluation of her and to ask you for more information about her."

I went immediately to the hospital and was met by a team of three nurses. They thanked me for coming and hoped I did not think they were being silly by calling me in for an evaluation. It seemed to them that Sister Taylor's conversation was not making sense that morning.

Sister Taylor had asked for her stuff. When they brought her clothes to her, she looked for the little sack she wore around her neck. Retrieving my card, she insisted on them calling me.

When I walked into her room, Sister Taylor was sitting on the side of the bed, fully clothed and ready to go home. (I still didn't know where home was.) After visiting with her, I concluded that she was acting normal and returned for my meeting with the nurses. I could add no new information, and they had made all the arrangements for her to go home.

Shortly after the hospital incident I moved to California. I've thought of her several times, and when I do questions fill my mind. You know, questions like you are having about her right now.

She came to the last service I had at the church. We parted with, "I'll see you later." I watched as she disappeared into the darkness, pulling her little red wagon with the large red reflectors, and wondered when and where we would meet again. Heaven? That would be excellent!

I have one regret. I did not tell her of the contribution she made to my life and the impact she made on my ministry. At the time, it didn't seem necessary. If she only knew . . .

Father, You know better than anyone that some of Your children have little of this world's goods. But, You also know that many of the rest of us fail to value and appreciate what is truly important. Thank You for using people like Sister Taylor to correct our perspectives. Amen.

Chapter 5

FROM ALCOHOL TO ALLELUIA

"My husband wanted me to call you and ask if you would pray for a man that is a drunk and has been for 12 years."

Her words were still occupying first place in my thoughts as I parked in front of their house in the flats, a somewhat run-down neighborhood in the southeast part of Oklahoma City. She was sitting on the front porch—unkempt, embarrassed, worried, and hurting—both physically and emotionally.

My heart went out to this woman as soon as I noticed she had only one foot. The other had been amputated about midway to her knee. I saw no aids for getting around—no wheelchair, walker, or even a crutch. As I approached the gate I tried to imagine what Christ would do if He were in my shoes. When I fumbled with the gate latch she said, "Please, don't come in."

I introduced myself as the pastor and she interrupted me. "I know. I called you. My husband wanted me to call, but he is not here now, so please don't come in. Just leave."

When I turned to walk away I heard a loud noise coming from inside the small house. It sounded like something, or someone, had fallen. Very slurred speech followed the noise, "Is that the preacher?"

The figure of a man appeared in the open doorway. He was trying to steady himself by holding onto the door, but was slowly sinking down to the floor. Finally, he looked at me from his sprawled position, and muttered a garbled request for prayer.

This was my first meeting with Omer King. A wave of anger mixed with compassion washed over me. I was angry at the liquor industry and all their pretty, enticing advertisements. Yet, I felt compassion for Omer—one of millions who had been deceived and destroyed by alcohol.

Mrs. King sat crying. Shame and embarrassment were etched on her face. "I am sorry I lied to you," she choked. "Please forgive me for lying to you—I didn't want you to see him like this." Her predicament and honesty touched me deeply.

Omer raised his head to look at me and once again slurred a request for prayer. Both of his eyes were red and the right one was turned permanently away from the left, twitching slightly. I looked him in the eye, as best I could, and refused to pray for him. I only promised to come back at another time.

Amazingly, my words seemed to spark something in Omer. Rising to his feet, he stumbled through the doorway onto the porch. As I turned to walk away, I heard him say, "My old Daddy was a Free Will Baptist preacher, and he would pray for anyone, at any time, under any condition!"

Continuing to walk toward the car, I realized that I heard and understood every word he spoke. (To this day, I still wonder if God cleared up his voice so I would truly hear what he said.) Momentarily thinking I had been too hasty in telling him I would not pray for him, I stopped. I turned back just in time to see him slump down on the floor, closing his eyes in a drunken slumber.

I kept my promise. I was at Omer's house at just past 7:00 a.m. the next day—about the time Mrs. King said Omer usually came home from working the night shift. I was there waiting and wondering, not knowing what to expect. I sat in my car, thumbing through my Bible still searching for the right passage of Scripture to use in praying for a drunken man. I wish I could say I was praying, but my only thoughts were of the previous day's scene.

This time, though, the setting had changed. Mrs. King was not in her chair. How did she get into the house? Visions of her crawling into her home flashed through my mind.

Just then, my thoughts were interrupted by the appearance of a uniformed man walking toward my car, head down, as though he was deep in thought. The man wore the uniform of a security guard, complete with a gun. Though I could not see his face, there was something about him that caused me to think I had seen him before.

Having turned my eyes back to my Bible, I was surprised to hear someone speak. "Good morning." I lifted my eyes to see Omer King standing beside my car. He was smiling, his left eye looking straight at me, his right eye looking north and twitching slightly.

"Get out and come in," Omer said. "I knew you would be here waiting for me."

I followed Omer to the porch where we sat down on the steps. Neither of us said a word. The silence between us grew until both of us were uncomfortable. Finally, he spoke.

"I don't know where to begin. I'm a drunk—have been for 12 years. Oh, I drank before then, but I have been drunk—I mean *drunk*—every day for the past 12 years. I guess there is no hope for me. I've prayed many times, but God never answered my prayers. Does He care about me? Has he given up on me?"

I turned to look at him. Tears dripped off his face and fell to the step beneath his feet. I wanted to say something, but what? My thoughts turned to the promise Jesus gave His servants. "Take no thought how or what ye shall speak: for it shall be given you in that same hour what ye shall speak" (Matthew 10:19b).

After what seemed like an hour of silence, I heard myself saying, "Omer, I remember reading some Scriptures in the Old Testament about the thoughts God had toward some other people. I'd like to share them with you . . . if I can only find them. They might help."

After a quick search I located Jeremiah 29:11-13. I read the words to him: "For I know the thoughts that I think toward you, saith the LORD, thoughts of peace, and not evil, to give you an expected end. Then shall ye call upon me, and ye shall go and pray unto me, and I will hearken unto you. And ye shall seek me, and find me, when ye shall search for me with all your heart."

After a long pause, I spoke. "Omer, you guessed there was no hope for you. And you want to know if God cares about you, and if He has given up on you. Well, according to these Scriptures, you guessed wrong. There is hope for you. God does care about you, and He hasn't given up on you. He is just a prayer away and He is waiting for you to get serious in your praying."

Omer got serious. He broke down. His tears and words flowed together in a prayer of deep repentance and faith toward God. Omer "prayed through"—through years of rebellion and drunkenness.

The spiritual transition was swift—Omer moved from darkness to light, from Satan's control to the Savior's control, from alcohol to alleluia, from the old life to the new. In a matter of moments he was "in Christ." Old things passed away and all things became new (2 Corinthians 5:17).

Omer looked at me. We both knew a miracle had taken place. He had been "born again" (John 3:3). "I must tell my wife!" he said eagerly.

At that moment we heard a joyful noise of laughter and weeping—praise and prayer—coming from inside the house. We entered through the door to find Mrs. King sitting on the floor rejoicing. Her crawl to the front porch had ended when she heard Omer praying. She prayed and waited. When the prayer ending and she heard us rejoicing, she joined in. It was a day she had longed to see.

As spiritual "babes in Christ," the King's first need was love and acceptance. Who would love and care for these spiritual babies? Was there a social agency somewhere? Would I, their pastor? I drove away with mixed emotions. I rejoiced that Omer and Mrs. King had been born again, but I resisted doing the nursery work of caring for these spiritual newborns. (It's only human to rejoice at births and still resist the rearing, you know.)

I did the natural thing. I consulted with my fleshly feelings. I didn't feel like I had the time or the energy to do the spiritual nursery work. I really felt like I should give myself to study and prayer. Someone else should take care of them—after all, I was the pastor. Why should I have to do this sort of stuff?

About then I remembered the words of my father, a preacher for over 60 years. "I learned a long time ago not to consult the flesh when it comes to serving God," he said. Those words prompted me to ask God to help me learn that lesson. My feelings began to ebb. I volunteered for "nursery" work. I knew then that love was not a feeling, but a choice. I had chosen to love and care for Omer and his wife even if I was the only person who did. (Thankfully, I wasn't.)

I realized later that the choice I made was very much like the choice my heavenly Father made in eternity past. Before the beginning of time, He chose to love the world and give His only Son so whoever believes in Him would not perish but have everlasting life (John 3:16). This same God can and will teach each of us how to love and receive love if we will allow Him (1 John 4:8b).

Now that I had volunteered for nursery work, where should I begin? I determined to stop by Omer's home the next day (Saturday) and offer them a ride to church. When I did so, Omer quickly accepted my offer. Mrs. King, however, declined. She said she had no way to get around. I assured her that I understood.

I drove away from their home anticipating the next day. It would be Omer's first time in church since his father's death nearly 20 years prior. It would also be his first time in church as a Christian. I could hardly wait!

Nine months later, the detective, Bill, and I drove separate cars to Mrs. King's house. I waited for Bill as he talked with his dispatcher. We walked slowly toward the front door of a small white house located on a quiet street in a nice neighborhood. The house was little, but it looked warm, cozy, and inviting. I could not keep from thinking that this was definitely a move up from where Omer and Mrs. King lived in the flats.

Light leaked around the edges of the drawn drapes and I wondered if Mrs. King was still up, or if she slept with a nightlight. Everything was so quiet and peaceful. I regretted having to interrupt the tranquility with bad news. Once again, I realized that pastors are not always the bearers of good news.

I took a deep breath and knocked on the door. Almost immediately Mrs. King responded.

"Who is it?" she asked.

"The pastor," I replied.

I could hear a shuffling sound as Mrs. King moved from the bed to her wheelchair—quite an accomplishment for a woman who had by then lost both legs to disease. I then heard her making her way to the door, the rattle of the door chain, followed by the clicking sound of the door locks. I prayed for words to tell her about Omer.

Mrs. King opened the door and looked beyond me at the detective. She rolled her wheelchair back as we entered the living room. Pointing to a couch, she invited us to sit down. As we sat down, I introduced Bill.

Mrs. King turned her chair to face me. Our eyes met.

"Pastor, which one of my boys is it this time?" (She had two sons and both were alcoholics.) I could say nothing. Her eyes filled with tears and she cried, "Oh, my God . . . not Omer! Please . . . not Omer!"

I was still searching for the right words when she spoke again.

"It is Omer, isn't it? Pastor, is he hurt? Is he dead?"

I nodded. Grief overwhelmed her. I felt I should say something, but I could think of nothing to say. I stood, put my arms around her shoulders, and we cried together.

Bill excused himself and left, saying something about finishing the paperwork later. I learned there are times when tears and touch are needed more than words.

Mrs. King calmed somewhat and we began to talk. We relived her last evening with Omer. It had been a joyful time. She had prepared the evening meal and packed snacks for Omer to take to work. Earlier that day Omer had picked up a picture of the two of them from the studio. It was their first time to have a picture made by a professional photographer and it was an excellent photo of them both. This picture would now be her most cherished possession.

Mrs. King spoke, "Pastor, tell me what you know about Omer's death."

"Omer arrived early for his night shift," I began. "He visited with the guard he was relieving. As his starting time drew near he excused himself for his prayer time. When he didn't return to begin his shift the guard he was relieving went looking for him. The guard found him at his favorite place for prayer. He was between the boilers and the wall. He was still in a kneeling position, leaning against the wall."

Mrs. King was silent for a long while before saying, "Pastor, I can't live without Omer."

"Can't, or don't want to live without him?" I asked.

"I don't want to live without him," she replied.

This feeling of despair would intensify. I was

frightened by what I heard and troubled by the look in Mrs. King's eyes.

Mrs. King did not want to live without Omer. She wanted to die. And she wondered why God didn't take her instead of him.

As I listened to her recount her physical condition and dependency on others, I knew living and dying were not new thoughts to her. I encouraged her to talk. She told of feelings of uselessness and how she had no one and nothing for which to live. She even told how on various occasions she had contemplated taking her own life. Only the fear of botching the attempt and the terror of standing before God in judgment prevented her from committing suicide.

Finally, she stopped talking and fixed her eyes on the floor. I could see her sinking into a pattern of bad thoughts. I waited several minutes before asking her to tell me more.

"Tell me about some of your good times," I asked.

Her thoughts began to change and as she raised her eyes to meet mine I could see a smile stretching her lips and her eyes sparkling in a dance of joy. Her hands slowly rose from her lap to form a cone. The dread had passed, at least for the present. She shifted slightly in her chair and I could see the results of her recollection of good times and thinking good thoughts.

Again, I encouraged her to talk—asking her to tell me about the things she remembered at that very moment. As I suspected, at the very moment she was thinking about Omer's conversion to Christ and her own spiritual renewal and the joyful times the two of them had together. The last nine months had been sheer bliss. For the first time in many years she had felt loved and appreciated—like a real wife. Then she added, "Now, Omer is dead."

"Omer is very much alive," I countered. "Only the body in which he lived for a time has died. Omer is enjoying that abundant life which Christ came to give to all who receive Him as Savior."

I went on to explain that life is more than body. Our bodies may be healthy or diseased, old or young, able or disabled. They may serve us well or not at all, but they are like a tent—a temporary dwelling place—until God moves us into the one He has prepared for us. Our bodies, though fashioned by God in our mother's womb and a marvelous work, wonderfully made, are still just flesh and blood. They were never intended to be our permanent dwelling place and they will never enter Heaven.

Even though we may abuse and pollute these bodies, when we turn to God in repentance and faith in Jesus Christ they can become (and do become) the temple of God. Imagine, God living in our tent with us! Incredible! (See 1 Corinthian 3:16-20.) Whether our bodies are young or old, weak or strong, whole or partial, God still lives within us. Our disabilities and weaknesses, though a bother to us, are opportunities for God to give us grace sufficient to meet our need and demonstrate His power (2 Corinthians 12:9).

In reality, we all live in perishing bodies—some in more advanced stages than others. Eventually, in God's timing and plan, we will move out of our present body into a new one, which He has prepared for us. (See 1 Corinthians 15:1-58 and 2 Corinthians 5:1-10.) That will be glory! Literally.

Regardless of the shape, size, or condition of our body, life is sacred. Life is a gift from God. We are to live for Him (Colossians 3:17, 23-24). Though we may think we have nothing, or no one for which to live, we always have HIM—the One who gave us life.

We may think our body to be useless and worthless to others and ourselves. Think again. Your body is your temporary home—your home away from home. And there is no body that God would not be pleased to live in and use for His glory. It is our privilege to invite Him in and to present our body to Him as a dwelling place (Romans 12:1-2).

Omer's body was abused and weakened by alcohol. But when given the opportunity, God moved in and only eternity will reveal the full impact Omer made on his friends, relatives, and church family. Omer's memorial service was attended by one of the largest crowds the church we ever had for such an occasion. He lived just nine months after his conversion. He was saved just in the nick of time.

Mrs. King's body was weakened and mutilated by disease. But, when given the opportunity, God moved in and used her to touch her alcoholic son. Heaven only knows the extent of her impact on others. She only lived a few months after Omer's home-going. Today, they are both in Heaven and I am looking forward to seeing them when my time comes.

Remember Omer's two brothers who had given up on him and forbad him to call them or come near their places? They will get to see and talk with him again. They and their families were all saved shortly after Omer left for Heaven.

Remember Mrs. King's two alcoholic sons? I heard from one of them about a year after Mrs. King left for Heaven. The one I heard from had been saved, delivered from alcohol, and on his way to Heaven. I don't know about the other, but I think maybe he also has turned to God. The burden to pray for him was lifted from my heart many years ago.

How God used Omer and Mrs. King to bring their loved ones and others to Christ? Well, that's a story for another time.

Lord, You work in unexpected ways. You bring triumph out of tragedy and glory out of gloom. Tune our hearts to praise You in all things, believing that no person or circumstance is beyond Your redemptive power. Amen.

Chapter 6

TIME MATTERS

Do you remember your early experiences in learning to tell time? I can remember some of mine. Some of the first-if not the first-were at home, with my father as the teacher.

The ticking of an old Big Bend pocket watch fascinated me. Papa would hold it close to my ear, urging me to listen, while he recited a little rhyme: "Tick, tock, tick, tock, the mouse ran up the clock." He would never complete the rhyme, nor would he allow me to hold the watch. He called it his very valuable timepiece, emphasizing that it was not a toy for kids to play with. I got the point.

Mama used the old alarm clock-a Waltman, I think-to help me learn to tell time. Her emphasis was on the hands of the clock. She would ask me to tell her where the big hand was and then where the little hand was positioned. Then she would tell me the time of day, thus beginning to teach me to tell time. One day I would have my own alarm clock and "valuable timepiece." But learning the value of time would come later.

I was soon to learn there was much more to time than just telling the time of day. Papa, like a true preacher man, would make my ears ring with statements I didn't understand-nor particularly care about. He would say, often very early in the day, "To everything there is a season, and a time to every purpose under heaven," quoting from Ecclesiastes 3:1. Sometimes he would continue quoting, telling about a time to be born, to die, to plant, to pluck up, to kill, to heal, to break down, to build up, to weep, to laugh, to mourn, to dance, to cast away stones, to gather stones, to embrace, to refrain from embracing, to get, to lose, to keep, to cast away, to rend, to sew, to keep silence, to speak, to love, to hate, a time to make war, and a time for peace (verses 2-8). (Yes, he knew this and many more passages of Scripture by heart.)

It was obvious to me that something was missing. There was no time to play! At that time in my life, playing was my passion. In time, I would have other passions. In more time, I would yield to the call of God on my life. Ministry-preaching, evangelizing, and pastoring-would become my strongest passion of all. And, in ministry, I would learn even more about time and timing.

In 1952, I received my first invitation to a full-time pastorate. I said yes, but I did not know what I was saying yes to. Looking back, though, I would do it all over again.

To me, accepting that church meant I would be living in a rent-free parsonage, preaching three times a week-twice on Sunday and once on Wednesday night. I would also be my own boss. I could do what I wanted, when I wanted, just because I wanted to. I must have sounded terribly brash to God. Good thing it was just between God and me.

However, as I would soon discover, a full-time pastor meant something quite different to the deacons and the church membership. From them I would hear that the church owned the house I lived in and paid my salary. I was there to look after the church business, minister to the needs of the membership, preach on Sundays, teach on Wednesday nights, contact the absentees, and evangelize in the community. It was quite a tall order for a 23 year-old with no experience as a pastor.

Where would I ever find the time to do all these things? I tried to recall some of my early instruction, but try as I might, I could not remember any of those lessons that addressed the situation I was now facing. In fact, the only thing I could remember about those days that had anything to do with time were the words Papa spoke when he called me in the mornings.

"Get out of that bed!" he would say. "Breakfast is about ready, and besides more people have died in bed than anywhere else!" Somehow that early morning greeting never failed to get me up and going. It was strange, but just remembering those words made me realize a pastor had to get up and get going. Thanks to Papa, I became an early riser. Decades later, the early morning hours are still my best time.

However, just getting up and going would not accomplish my work. I would need some type of schedule and I soon discovered my schedule would need some fine-tuning to keep the day's rhythm. And, to my surprise, a bedridden saint would be an important part of this tune-up.

Sister Smith had been ill for a very long time and confined to her bed for over a year. Her physical condition was no longer on the front burner of our church's ministry. In fact, her name did not appear on the prayer list and she was only mentioned occasionally by some of the women in private conversation. New people did not know of her, even when they heard her name. Even I, the new pastor, had not so much as heard of her before a deacon asked me if I had been to see her.

When I discovered that she lived with her daughter only a short distance from the church I felt terrible. My mind swirled with questions. Why did this deacon wait until now to tell me about this poor lady? How could I face her with the fact that no one told me about her? How could such a thing happen in a church family? Was she forgotten intentionally? Was it out of neglect? How was it that a pastor, her Sunday School teacher, the women's auxiliary-seemingly the entire church family-could just busy themselves with ministry and miss an opportunity to brighten the day of a bedridden saint?

Monday afternoon I went to see Sister Smith. Stopping in front of her house, I paused for prayer before getting out of my car. I might have delayed exiting the car even longer, but I saw a curtain move at the front window and thought someone inside was watching me.

Mentally and emotionally I was struggling with this aspect of ministry. I felt so helpless, not knowing what to say or do for a person who was confined to bed and battling a terminal illness. I was soon to learn that Sister Smith herself would help me in this area.

Remembering that I was representing Jesus Christ-making this visit on His behalf-I straightened up my walk and put a smile on my face as I walked the few feet from the car to the front door. I knocked on the door and waited.

A gracious lady opened the door, greeting me as "Pastor." How she knew I was a pastor was a mystery to me. (I was reminded again that in a small church situated in a small community, most every move the pastor makes is known and reported.) Opening the door wider, she invited me into the house.

"Mother and I have been expecting you," she said, "ever since Ruth [the deacon's wife] called early this morning. This way please, Mother is in the front bedroom."

I followed, expecting to be scolded-and rightly so- for not coming sooner. To my surprise, I was greeted most warmly by a bedridden figure, smiling and beckoning me to come closer. I took her extended hand in mine, our eyes met, and I knew she was sincere when she said, "Thank you for coming. I am blessed just to have one of God's preacher boys in my home."

I looked at my watch, remembering the words of my mentor, "Most of the time, a ten minute visit is a sufficient amount of time to spend at the bedside of the ill. A pastor should never wear out his welcome." Time was passing quickly. Another ten minutes and I would be going.

"Sister Smith," I forced myself to say, "would you like for me to read Scripture and have prayer before I go?"

"Go? You just got here. What do you mean, before you go?"

"I don't have much time today," I said, "but I will be back."

My excuses didn't hold water with Sister Smith. Her voice grew firm as she told me to sit down.

"Pastor, you have just as much time as anyone-we all have the same amount. God has given us 24 hours a day. Evidently, you are not using your time right."

Ouch! This was the first in a series of lessons on the use of time that Sister Smith was to teach me and it was a painful way to begin. Although this bedridden saint did not know she was actually teaching during our visits, I soon learned she had much more to share with me both in word and example.

Sister Smith had my attention. She spoke of the value of time and the importance of "redeeming the time" as Paul had taught (Ephesians 5:16; Colossians 4:5). Outwardly, I nodded my head in agreement. Inwardly, I determined to study those verses for their correct application.

Later, when I was alone in my office, I began my study. Within the week I had concluded that Sister Smith was on the right track. I certainly could improve the way I used my time. I soon became eager for another visit with Sister Smith. I wanted to know just how a person in her circumstance used her time. Given her physical limitations, how could she redeem the time? Frankly, I didn't think it was possible, but somehow I believed she did. I had to find out.

The day came for my return visit. I prayed before going, asking God for courage to follow through with my planned inquiry. In one sense, it was none of my business. But in another sense, the way she used her time just might be an inspiration to me.

Upon my arrival at Sister Smith's I was greeted first by a young man. He introduced himself as a grandson who came to do Granny's yard. He had the appearance of an industrious young man who used his time wisely. Sure enough, even before I asked, he voluntarily told me of his Granny's teaching on the use of time. He even laid out his plan for the day. I would later discover he followed her teaching closely.

"Nice meeting you, Pastor," he said. "You have a good day and a good visit with Granny. I'll see you around."

With those words he was on his way. I walked toward the house thinking he had just given me a push toward having a good day . . . and it seemed so easy for him to do. Wow!

At the door I was again greeted warmly by the daughter and taken to Sister Smith's room. We exchanged greetings and chatted for a few minutes about the church, the weather, and other such things. All the while, I was thinking about my main reason for coming. Finally, I could not wait any longer.

"Sister Smith," I blurted out abruptly, "I've been thinking about our talk the other day and you telling me I just wasn't using my time right. I would like to know how you use your time. It might help me to improve."

Sister Smith laughed heartily. "Pastor, you are probably thinking that an old, bedridden lady like me has no real life." Still chuckling, she went on, "Well, quite the contrary. I am very much alive. It is only my body that is bedridden, and I gave my body to the Lord many years ago. It belongs to Him and whatever He does with it, or permits to be done to it, I accept. I've learned not to question Him or blame Him for my physical conditions over which I have no control. I just try to remember Paul's experience and try to claim the sufficiency of God's grace, as promised to him." (She was referring to 2 Corinthians 12:1-10; particularly verse 9: "And he said unto me, My grace is sufficient for thee: for my strength is made perfect in weakness. Most gladly therefore will I rather glory in my infirmities, that the power of Christ may rest upon me.")

A holy hush enveloped the room. I knew I was in the presence of God and that He was pleased with what He heard from His bedridden child. She was right. Sister Smith was God's child, and in His time He would give her a new body suited for her heavenly home.

As Sister Smith continued to speak I learned of her once-active life. She had worked in the local school system, cared for her family, taught Sunday School, and still had time for other church and community projects.

"How did you ever manage to have time to do all of those things and still have a life for yourself?" I asked.

She laughed again. "It was fun," she replied. "Not all of the time, of course, there was a sprinkling of times when it wasn't. But to answer your question about a life of my own, I did not live for myself. I lived first for my Lord, my husband, my children, my church, and other people and things came last."

Sister Smith went on to tell me of first giving herself to Christ every morning when she awakened. Then she sought to do His will for the day in the matters awaiting her attention. She daily submitted her "To Do" list to God and asked for His help in arranging and accomplishing the work. She wanted her work to be a service to God and for Him to be glorified. Having done this, she got started and followed through on each task.

I could see she was getting tired, but I couldn't resist asking if she still did these things. She did-with some minor changes, of course. When she awakened she first committed herself afresh to the Lord and then prayerfully asked Him to reveal His will for her day. The list she submitted to the Lord had changed somewhat. It now consisted of medications, baths, meals, Scripture readings, prayer times, phone calls, inspirational readings, correspondence, witnessing, and visiting with guests.

One of the most touching things she talked about was how irritable she was at times and her attitude toward her caregivers. Her dependence upon others was hard to accept and turn over to the Lord. Relief came when she could honestly pray for herself and her caregivers. She admitted to repenting and apologizing often.

I was especially impressed with her prayer time. She prayed for me and for the church. Her caregivers, including her doctor and pharmacist, were also included in her prayers. Her love for her family and missionaries were likewise evidenced in the time she spent interceding for them. It seemed as though no one was left out. And, I learned, there were days when she prayed for the entire day. That day, we prayed together before I left.

Sister Smith long ago entered the presence of her Lord. But my visits with her yielded much more than I ever expected and I have incorporated some of her teachings in my own prayer life. I will never forget the bedridden saint who taught me how to use my time, or the emphasis she placed on prayer.

Maybe when I get to heaven I will get to tell her just how she enriched my life and that I passed on to you the things she taught me. On second thought, why don't you just tell her yourself?

Father, time is Your unique gift to Your children, for You live beyond the confines of minutes, hours, and days. Help us to make the most of this gift and to use it in ways that please You and further Your purposes on this earth, until the day when we join you in the eternal now of Your presence. Amen.

Chapter 7

THE MIDNIGHT WITNESS

While serving as pastor of a church in Oklahoma City, I was contacted by Brother Gilbert, a personal friend and pastor of a church in Duncan, Oklahoma. He invited me to serve as their evangelist for a one-week revival meeting.

I would have no daytime duties other than to pray and study in preparation for the evening services, he said. Gilbert offered to provide accommodations for me at his home, the church, or a local motel. He also said that if I preferred I could commute to the services from my home in Oklahoma City, or, he joked, I could even take all four options. After some prayer, I opted to commute to each service from my home. This would allow me to have more alone time for prayer and study in my own office where I kept my tools (books) within arm's reach.

The revival meeting began on Monday night. I was surprised at the attendance. Over 100 people gathered for that service, expecting God to do a work in their midst. They weren't disappointed. When the invitation to come forward was given, three adults came forward to receive Jesus Christ as Savior. Several more would follow during the week. Christians came, too, in good numbers, to pray for family and friends who didn't know Christ.

By Friday night the pastor and people were talking about continuing the meeting into the next week or as long as interest prevailed. Papa, a highly effective evangelist in his day, used to call that kind of meeting an "open end" revival, meaning it would go on as long as God continued to pour out His blessings upon it.

By week's end, the church had requested that I stay over and preach the following week. I agreed to return on Sunday night, explaining my desire to preach at my home church on Sunday morning. They agreed.

The next week, revival fires continued to burn brightly. We closed the meeting on Saturday night of the second week and enjoyed a social hour following the service. It was a celebration time with the new Christians who had received Christ during the 14 nights of the meeting.

Finally, I headed for home. Sunday was coming. I looked at my watch. It was a little past 11:00 p.m. I decided to use the drive time to pray and seek God's leading for the Sunday message at my own church. My body was tired, more so than I realized. It had been a blessed week, but a very hard week on me physically and emotionally. My commute was over 100 miles per night. During the day I had prayed and studied for the night service and extended pastoral care to my own flock. I was drained, but I refused to complain. Instead, I gave thanks to God for the opportunity to serve, for the people who had been saved during the meeting, and for the very generous honorarium the church had given me.

Nevertheless, my body was tired and needing sleep. *Only a few more miles and I'll be home.* That was the last thought I remember before drifting off to sleep. The thud of the tires leaving the pavement jolted me awake. I struggled with the wheel to turn the car back onto the road. Somehow, by the grace of God, I managed to correct it and avoid an accident. "Thank You, Lord," I whispered, and promised myself I would stop at the next coffee shop to get awake.

The coffee shop came much sooner than I expected. The close call had left me so wide-awake, I even considered driving on. At that moment, I felt like I could drive forever. But, I remembered my promise and pulled into the parking lot. Getting out of my car, I looked at my watch and noticed it was nearly midnight. I entered the coffee shop and looked around. Four people were sitting in a round booth.

"Sit where you want," the waitress called out. I selected a booth several feet from where the others sat. I had my Bible with me and was about to review my plans for the morning message when one of the men in the round booth began swearing-taking God's name in vain. He continued talking loudly, repeating his oaths. One of the ladies who sat with him tried to quiet him down, but he turned on her and blasted her with vulgarity. "I'll talk as loud as I want and any way I want!" he declared. Then he proved his point by continuing on with his diatribe.

I quickly grew restless and decided to finish my coffee and leave. That's when I felt an inner nudge. I knew that feeling. It was the Holy Spirit and He wanted me to witness to the man.

Who? Me? But, I just stopped to wake up, not to witness! I argued silently.

But aren't you already awake after that little incident back down the road? I had to admit I was.

Weren't you the one who thought you could drive forever back then? Well, yes, I guess I did.

After all, were all those things that happened just a coincidence? Okay, okay! Maybe I was here for this very purpose. Although I didn't realize it, maybe I did stop to speak to someone about Christ instead of just to wake up.

I prayed again, asking God to show me how to go about it, if He was indeed the One behind all of this.

My coffee cup was empty and the group in the booth was leaving. I paid for my coffee and followed them out the door into the parking lot.

"Excuse me! Excuse me, please," I said.

They all stopped and turned to face me.

"I overheard you speaking of my Father tonight. I'm not sure which one of you spoke of Him and I am curious as to how well you know Him."

A puzzled expression crept across their faces. Then one of them spoke.

"I don't believe I know you," he said. "Who are you? And who is your father?"

"God is my Father-my heavenly Father," I replied. "You spoke freely and often of Him tonight. You even asked Him to damn several things, which as you probably know, He is certainly capable of doing. Do you know Him?"

The man who spoke was now left alone with me in the parking lot. His friends had walked to their car. Finally, he spoke again.

"Thank you for stopping me," he said, to my

surprise. "I do know your Father. I once knew Him very well. I was a Christian for many years, and served on a church board. Then the devil got into our home. My wife left me. I blamed God for my troubles and walked out on Him."

By now his eyes were filled with tears and his voice cracked with emotion. I asked him to acknowledge his sins to God and return to Him, right then and there. Unfortunately, he refused. But he did promise he would do so on Sunday, in his old home church. I could only hope he would keep his promise.

We prayed together before going our separate ways. He joined his friends. I returned to my car and headed for home. My midnight witness was finished. Sunday was coming.

Father, sometimes when we least expect it, You call. In the most unlikely of circumstances, through the people we would least imagine, we sometimes hear Your voice. Tune our ears to hear and our hearts to respond to You. Amen.

Chapter 8

THE SEVERITY OF GOD

While preaching through Genesis, I came upon a scene in chapter 38 which reminded me of what I understand to be the severity of God. This is a side of God many know nothing about, and only a few preachers will preach about.

Er and Onan, sons of Judah, grandsons of Jacob, were slain by the Lord. We are not told much about their wickedness, but both did evil in God's sight and He killed them (Genesis 38:6-10). What a shock it must have been to Tamar, Er's wife, and the rest of their family and friends. Here today-gone today. No doubt, these survivors wondered who would be next.

I do not think the deaths of Er and Onan were so-called mercy killings. Nor, do I believe God unjustly took their lives. I believe it was life's payday for them. They simply collected their wages for living a sinful life (Romans 6:23a).

I base this opinion on the sovereignty of God and the testimony of Scripture. The Bible speaks of a way that seems right to man, but its end is death (Proverbs 14:12; 16:25). It also speaks of those who are often reproved or admonished but stubbornly refuse to repent and are suddenly destroyed ". . . and that without remedy" (Proverbs 29:1).

Some would say, "But we live in the day of grace!" implying that the severity of God would never be exercised against anyone in this day. But, I would answer, God does not change (Malachi 3:6). And, we also have an incident recorded for us in the New Testament—a scene which I believe can only be an act of divine judgment—in which the severity of God falls upon a man and his wife and they pay for their deceit with their lives (Acts 5:1-11).

My father, Joseph Elza ("Elzie") Yandell, told of an incident that seemed to be a modern-day illustration of the severity of God. Papa had been preaching nightly beneath a brush arbor in eastern Oklahoma. A brush arbor was a crude temporary meeting place that consisted of little more than an awning of wood, tree limbs, and brush. It had no exterior walls, but it did offer a little shelter beneath which were fashioned some crude wooden benches on which the congregation sat.

Each service was preceded by a grove prayer meeting in which the Christian men and women of that community were praying for those who were unsaved. Attendance at the "revival" was growing nightly. Many were receiving Christ as Savior.

On a Thursday night, a family that was not known for attending church came in a wagon pulled by a team of mules. The woman and her children made their way under the arbor to look for a seat. Seats were scarce, so some men stood and offered them a place to sit.

The woman was so caught up in the service that she appeared as though she was in a trance. She sat with rapt attention, seemingly hungry for the words that were being spoken. The family returned the next night, and the next. On the third night of their attendance (Saturday) the woman went forward to the altar to repent of her sins and receive Jesus Christ as her Savior. Her husband had not, on any night, come under the arbor, but witnesses said he had come close enough to see his wife go to the altar.

On Sunday night, the family returned again for the fourth time. As always, Papa preached with much fervor. When the invitation was given, the woman again came to the altar. This time she was praying for her husband. He had not received her conversion very well, so she asked Papa and all the Christians there to pray for her husband. They did.

Papa stood to continue the invitation. Sensing the leadership of the Holy Spirit, he went to the woman's husband to give him a personal invitation to come and receive Christ as Savior. Witnesses reported the man was less than kind in his response to Papa's entreaty.

"Preacher, you got my woman up there and made a fool out of her and you are not going to make a fool out of me!"

"My dear sir," Papa replied, "I will be praying for you." Then he returned to the altar to pray for the man.

Soon Papa's prayer was interrupted by a man tapping him on the shoulder. "Brother Yandell," he said, "the man you was talking with has fallen to the ground-slain in the Spirit!"

Papa rushed to the man. He was dead.

Some said he died of a heart attack. Others said

his death was caused by some kind of a chemical upset in his body. Papa believed it was divine judgment-the severity of God had fallen upon him (Romans 11:22No one knows for sure what happened. But they knew one thing-he died without a Savior.

Father, Your power is both a comfort and a terror to us, for our lives-both here and in eternity-are in Your hands. Give us mercy, Lord, not justice. For we deserve Your wrath, but we rejoice in Your grace, proud to be a fool for you. Amen.

Chapter 9

WHEN LIFE TURNS TRAGIC

A quadriplegic! Bobby is a quadriplegic? I couldn't believe it. What went wrong?

I remembered Bobby as an oversized 14-year-old boy. His father and mother were devoted Christians. Bobby's dad was a hard-working minister who worked during the week as a carpenter and ministered in small churches on Sundays. Bobby's parents spoke often of how God had blessed them both materially and spiritually. Now Bobby was paralyzed.

As my parents told me of Bobby's accident, I tried to mentally catch up. During my tour of duty in the U.S. Navy, a lot of changes had taken place. Bobby had grown from the awkward kid I knew to a tall and handsome young man. At just 15 years of age, he said God had called him to preach the gospel of Jesus Christ. His plans included graduating from high school and going on to Bible College in preparation for a lifetime of service for God.

On a certain Sunday, Bobby's father asked him to speak in his stead at the small church he was pastoring. (An unusual, but not unheard of opportunity in the small churches of that day.) Bobby's message was powerful and he was an instant hit with the church family—especially the youth.

A family of the church invited Bobby and all the teens from the church to their home for lunch. It was a fun time and by the time lunch was over the kids had arranged a swimming party for the afternoon. Bobby agreed to go, but only as a spectator, because he had not brought clothes for swimming. However, someone came up with a pair of jeans Bobby could wear and he consented to join them after all.

When they arrived at the old swimming hole, the kids made a mad rush for the water; everyone was scrambling to be the first one in. Bobby—a tall, lean, athletic type—dove into the water first. Tragically, the water wasn't deep enough for diving and he struck his head, breaking his neck. In an instant, the handsome young man became a quadriplegic. He would never recover from the accident.

My parents told me that Bobby wanted to see me. I lived 200 miles away, but sent word by my folks that I would come to see him in the near future. Within a few weeks, I made the long drive to see Bobby. All I had been told about Bobby did not prepare me for this visit. It was my first time to visit a paralyzed individual. I was fearful of saying or doing the wrong thing, thinking I might add to the mental and emotional pain he was suffering. The drive passed quickly and I was soon parked in front of his house . . . cold feet and all.

Bobby's mother invited me into the house and immediately took me to his room. He greeted me with a booming voice, as though he was trying to compensate for his condition. I walked to the side of his hospital bed knowing he could not shake hands and wondering what my next move should be. He seemed to sense my awkwardness, saying with a smile, "I'll meet you part way." He lifted his right hand a little and I cupped it in mine. We both knew it was more than a mere meeting of the hands, it was a meeting of the hearts. Though I was a few years older than Bobby and we had not spent much time together, we were close in spirit.

The afternoon passed before either of us was ready to end our visit. I had a 200-mile drive to make and felt I should be getting on the road. I stood and asked that the two of us pray for one another. Bobby said, "First, I want to tell you something. I think it is the real reason why I wanted, and needed, to talk with you."

I listened as Bobby told me of the Sunday he preached, and the afternoon swimming party—much of what my parents had already told me. Then he went on to tell me about his injury and what it had done to him as a person.

It had been two very long years for him. Just 24 months ago he was a young man of vigor and vitality. Then, he weighed around 200 pounds. Now, he weighed only 120. He had only a slight mobility in his right arm and hand. His eyes filled with tears as he said, "I'm helpless."

Like most young people, Bobby wanted his space. He resented parental control and strained against their reins. On one occasion, he had even threatened them with, "Just wait until I'm 18. Things are gonna change then—I'm moving out." But, that was before his life took a tragic turn. In an instant, he had gone from pushing his parents for his freedom to do as he pleased to a complete and irreversible dependence upon them. Now he could do nothing for himself. He confessed that he had even considered suicide, but realized he could not even take his own life without their help, or that of someone else.

Bobby turned his eyes toward me and waited for my response. I tried to prepare myself for the worst possible question he could ask of me. Momentarily, my imagination went wild. I braced for a question he could never ask. I was needlessly fearful and worried over a situation that would never develop. (A lot like you may be feeling as you read these words.)

Bobby went on to tell of experiencing overwhelming boredom. His physical condition brought on mental weariness. He felt sorry for himself. He told of growing tired of hearing the Scriptures read and the praying of prayers that seemed to offer him only a false hope and fake optimism. His number of visitors had dwindled and those who kept coming were uninteresting—parroting meaningless phrases and words.

In his desperate fight to cope with boredom, Bobby asked for a television and cigarettes. His parents purchased a small television and mounted it on the wall for his viewing. His dad gave him a pack of Camel cigarettes. These diversions helped with his boredom for a while, but the television also led him to his greatest delusion and disappointment.

Every week, Bobby watched the programs of televangelists and so-called "faith healers." He became enamored with the faith healers and watched as people threw crutches away to run across the stage. He heard some testify of excruciating pain that suddenly went away during the prayer and touch of the healer's hand.

Others were wheeled across the platform in wheelchairs. At the healer's command they would abandon their chairs—running down the platform steps into the aisles among the congregation. Week after week Bobby watched the shows. Slowly, he began to believe in the faith healers. His favorite one told a touching story of his own healing when he was just a young boy and of God calling him to a healing ministry for others. Bobby was impressed.

In time, the so-called faith healer announced he was coming to Dallas, Texas (approximately 150 miles from where Bobby lived) for a one-week healing crusade. He urged the sick, crippled, and paralyzed to come for healing. Citing the story of the friends who removed the roof of a house in order to get a paralyzed man to Jesus, the faith healer called on friends and families to do the same for their loved ones. He emphasized that the citywide campaign would only be for one week and urged people to come early.

Bobby wanted to go. He was desperate. He *would* go! But, it would require both an ambulance and plane.

Bobby's parents made arrangements to take him to the healing campaign. They hired an ambulance to transport him to the airport, chartered a small plane to fly him to Dallas, and arranged for another ambulance to take him to the location of the crusade. The cost was astronomical for a poor family, but they were doing whatever was necessary, just as the healer said.

When the family reached the crusade site they stood in awe. A large tent had been erected. Seating thousands, this tent would house the services. Smaller tents flanked the large one. In these smaller tents hundreds of people were being processed. Each sought a place in the healing lines that would form and move across the platform in front of the healer.

Bobby was placed in one of the small tents to be processed. A man came to fill out a registration card, recording Bobby's name, address, the type and length of his illness, and the status of his medical treatment. After completing the card, the man left saying someone would be in to see him.

No one came.

Bobby's place in the healing line never materialized, either. Neither the healer, nor one of his associates, ever came to see Bobby. His parents tried to ask questions and get someone to help Bobby, but their efforts were to no avail. The only prayers ever prayed for Bobby at that crusade were those of his father and mother who shared in his letdown. The family returned home, disillusioned and disappointed in so-called faith healers, but stronger and much wiser in the true faith and love of God.

Bobby's story was about over, but he wasn't quite finished.

"I know you have a long drive home and need to be on your way," he said, "but I want you to know that I am not bitter, nor do I blame God for my condition. I did a very stupid thing and my error has caused this [paralysis]. God has not left me. I sense His presence every day and night. Someday He will come for me and then I will be whole, in a body He has prepared for me. I will be with Him forever."

Bobby broke the somber mood with laughter. "I should have known that faith healer was a fake. He never healed anyone in the hospitals, malls, markets, or homes. Only on a platform under lights and before the TV cameras." At that we both laughed.

I had planned to see Bobby again, but before I did I received a call saying Bobby's Lord had come for him. Bobby was finally at home, a quadriplegic no more. His tragedy had been turned to triumph.

Father, deliver us from faith in men, but infuse us with faith in You. Let us learn to trust You for healing and for hope, as it brings glory to You. Amen.

Chapter 10

~

WILL YOU BE SAVED?

It was the early 1960's and I was the pastor of a church in Oklahoma City. I had just finished visiting the last person on my hospital visitation list and was making my way to the elevator for a quick exit for home. The day had been long and I was looking forward to an evening with my family.

As I approached the elevator I noticed a woman standing with her head bowed as though she was praying. She had not pushed either of the buttons for up or down. I pushed the down button and glanced toward her. It was then that I saw she was crying softly. I felt a little awkward as I decided whether or not to invade her world.

Before I could decide, she looked at me and spoke very softly, "I'm sorry." I managed to respond with "That's alright. May I be of help? I am a pastor."

"I don't think so," she replied. "I don't think anyone can help." Then she opened up a bit, "I am so burdened for my father," she said. "He is 85 years old and is seriously ill. The doctor said he only has a few days to live."

I asked if she had a pastor. She did. Then I asked if her father had a pastor. He did not. I offered to go see him, and waited for her response.

"Oh, I just don't know if you should or not," she responded. "Dad has run off my pastor and the hospital chaplain and forbidden them to return." She hesitated briefly, but then spoke with a new resolve, "Pastor, Dad is dying and he will go to Hell unless he repents and receives Jesus Christ as Savior. I just can't give up on him. If you will go see him, knowing he has already run two ministers off, I would appreciate it." I assured her I would go.

The relaxing evening I had looked forward to was not so relaxing after all. My mind kept going back to the conversation with a stranger burdened for her father-an old man dying lost. Would he be one saved as a firebrand plucked from the eternal fire? (Amos 4:11; Jude 23). I knew I had to join the team of Christians trying to reach the old man for Christ. Tomorrow I would take my turn.

Arriving at University Hospital around 2 p.m., I went immediately to room six where the elderly man lay inching his way toward death and judgment. He was alert and alone in the room. I approached his bedside and greeted him. "Hi, Bill," I said, not giving him my name. (He didn't ask for it, either.)

Bill and I chatted about the weather-a pretty, bright day outside. I commented on the brightness of his room and the flowers and cards he had received. Eventually, I ventured beyond the small talk.

"Bill, what brings you to the hospital?"

"I came here to die," he replied. "Just found out about it a little while ago. That's what the doctors say. Yup, came here to die."

Bill drifted off into his own thoughts, but my question brought him back to the moment.

"What then?" I asked.

"Don't know," he said, "I guess somebody will put me in a hole and shovel dirt on me. That's about all there is to it, ain't it?"

"Well, Bill, I wouldn't be too sure of that," I answered. "I've heard others say there was much more to dying than just being buried. I've heard that we have a spirit and a soul that lives on somewhere. I've heard that part of us never dies. Have you ever heard anything like that?"

"Yup. Heard that. Don't believe it. I think when you die, that's it. You're done for. You're through."

"Bill," I continued, "where did you hear about a man having a soul and a spirit that will live on somewhere?"

"At church."

"Tell me about it," I prompted.

"I used to go to church," he began, "even went down to the front to the altar. But it didn't take me long to find out they were all a bunch of hypocrites and crooks. The preacher was the worst one. My wife died believing that junk. She never gave up trying to get me to go back, and she even tried to get me to promise to come to her someday."

"Did you make her a promise?"

"No!" he replied with an expletive.

"Why?"

Bill never answered my question. Instead, he grew quiet, then his whole outward expression changed.

His face grew flushed and a wild look came to his eyes. His hands began to shake and suddenly he exploded in an emotional rage.

"You're a damn preacher!" he shouted. "Get out of my room and take your [expletive] God with you!"

I left his room weeping, not for myself, but for him and his family. In a small way, I felt the pain his daughter did, knowing he would probably die and go to Hell. But, like his daughter, I just couldn't give up on him. I had to try again.

The following day I returned to Bill's room. A notice to visitors hung on the door-"Family Members Only." What was I to do? I knocked lightly on the door and one of the daughters opened the door just a crack. She was the same woman I had met at the elevator and she was glad to see me.

Stepping out into the hallway she said, "Dad is weaker and restless. He is not doing well and the doctor says it is only a matter of hours before he goes." She began to cry. "We found your card on the stand. Thank you for coming to see him. He told us he ran you off when he realized you were a preacher. He said you were a nice guy, but sneaky-that you never admitted or denied you were a preacher."

We laughed together, seeing a little light of humor in a dark hour.

The other sisters joined us in the hospital hallway. The four of us talked and prayed together. We discussed if I should go in to see him. All agreed that I should, knowing I would probably be rejected. So the four of us went in together.

Bill turned his head to see who came in. He spotted me and said in the coldest way a man could possibly speak, "I told you to get out of my room and to take your [expletive] God with you! Now get out!"

I left as Bill mumbled more curse words with what strength he had left.

Bill's daughters followed me into the hallway where we prayed together. They expressed appreciation for my efforts. We said our goodbyes and I left.

Bill died the next day, without a Savior as far as I know. Still, I'm glad I tried.

I do not know what you think about God, but I do know what God thinks about you. He loves you and gave His only begotten Son to die for your sins so you may have eternal life instead of perishing in a Hell prepared for the devil and his "angels" or demons (John 3:16; Matthew 25:41).

Will you be saved? I sincerely hope so. But the longer you wait the more likely it is that you will not. Consider this: researchers report that 19 out of every 20 people who become Christians do so before they reach age 25. After 25 years of age, only one in 10,000 come to Christ. After 35 years of age, only one in 50,000. After 45, only one in 200,000. After 55, only one in 300,000. After age 65, only one in 500,000. And after 75 years of age, only one in 700,000 ever come to know Christ as Savior.

Will you be saved? Only if you respond to God's love with faith in Jesus Christ. We are saved by grace (God's love) through faith (in Jesus Christ). (See Ephesians 2:8-10.) God will save all who come to Him in this manner regardless of their age. There no better time than the present for you to invite Him into your life.

Jesus, they may someday say, "I wish I had listened," but may our friends never say, "I wish they had told me." Amen.

Chapter 11

A BLOODY GIFT

I was at work when the call came. Her voice sounded young. As she spoke I detected a lot of anxiety. I waited to see what was to come next.

Trying hard to be calm, she said, "Pastor, my father is in the University Hospital. He is 87 years old and he is having emergency surgery tonight. He needs blood donors and my cousin, who has been attending your church, told me to give you a call. She thought you might be able to help."

The woman went on to tell me that she lived out of town and had come home to do some wash and rest a bit, then she was planning to return to the hospital. I promised to try to get blood donors and asked permission to pray with her over the phone. She agreed, so we prayed together.

When we finished she was weeping softly. "Thank you," she said. Then she added, "Pastor, my father is not saved. Can you help? Daddy is a good man, but he is lost.

I don't want him to go to Hell when he dies. I don't think I could take that . . ."

Tears were now flowing freely and unashamedly. I thought of Jesus weeping over Jerusalem for very similar reasons (Matthew 23:37-38). I asked my caller if she was a Christian by spiritual birth. She was. We again prayed together for her father, believing God for his salvation and committing him to God's care and keeping.

After we hung up, I made a few phone calls and five people told me they would be glad to donate blood. I quickly rearranged my own schedule, locked the office door, and left immediately. In making my usual rounds of the hospitals to visit the sick I would go to Baptist Hospital first, then St. Agnes and Mercy hospitals, and finally end up at University Hospital about 4:30 p.m.

At the University Hospital information desk a cheerful lady in pink directed me to the second floor where the man's room was located. In those days, the hospital had its own blood bank and from where I was standing I could see the door to it. I decided to give a pint of blood before going up to see the patient.

It was after 5:00 p.m. when I stepped off the elevator. I walked to the end of the hallway and into a large room containing several beds that were separated only by thick blue curtains. I asked a nurse about the patient. She pointed toward a blue curtain that was drawn completely around a bed.

"They are preparing him for surgery," she said. "As soon as they are finished you may see him."

I prayed while I waited.

When they finished prepping him, I stepped inside the blue curtain and introduced myself to this total stranger. Other than being human, male, and dearly loved by God, we had nothing else in common.

"Who are you?" he asked.

"I'm a pastor," I replied.

"A what?"

"A pastor-you know, a preacher. I pastor a church."

"Oh," he said. "I went to church once when my baby daughter got married . . . ain't been back since."

All at once, his daughter pulled the curtain aside and stepped inside. "Daddy, I'm back!" she said cheerfully. Her father smiled and took her into his arms. After a long embrace, she straightened up, extended her hand toward me and said, "I'm the baby daughter. On my way up I stopped by the blood bank and they told me you gave blood for Daddy. Thank you!"

She turned toward her father. "Daddy, the pastor here gave blood for you a little while ago." The old man looked at me. A quizzical expression came across his face. Then he spoke.

"You gave blood for someone you didn't know- hadn't even met or seen?" he asked.

The daughter spoke up before I could answer, "That's not all, Daddy. He has five friends that are giving blood for you. We have enough for your surgery."

The old man was overwhelmed. We cried together. Through his tears the old man said, "I've never had anyone to give their blood for me before."

Sensing God's timing and the nudge of the Holy Spirit, I nervously replied, "I know of someone else who gave His blood for you."

"Who?" asked the old man.

"His name is Jesus. Would you like to know more about Him and how He gave His blood for you?"

When he answered yes, I began.

"The Bible says, 'the life of the flesh is in the blood.' We all know what that means. We must have blood flowing through our veins to continue living the natural or physical life. That's the reason for blood donors and blood transfusions."

The old man agreed, so I continued: "However, some may not know that the Bible says we also have a spiritual life to live. That is, within our body lives our spirit."

"I've never thought of it that way," he responded, "but I believe what the Bible says about it."

I went on to explain that our spirit is the part of us that continues as a being after our body dies. When our body dies, is buried, and returns to the dust, our spirit will continue to live in one of two places-Paradise or Hell.

"Paradise or Heaven," I explained, "is eternal life. It means living forever with Jesus Christ in a place He has prepared-a place that abounds with good things! But, Hell-which is eternal death-is a place of torment and unquenchable fire. It means being forever separated from Jesus Christ. The blood that flowed through the veins of Jesus Christ was the life of the incarnate Christ. The blood He shed was for the salvation of all. People give blood so others may live physically, but that's temporary. Jesus gave His blood that people may live spiritually, and that's eternal."

I stopped to ask my new friend if he understood what I was saying. He said that he did. So I ventured another question:

"Would you like to have eternal life?"

"More than anything else," was his reply.

I shared with him six steps to salvation that I have

shared with many others:

- Acknowledge that you are a sinner (Romans 3:23).
- Repent (turn away from) of your sins (Luke 13:3; Acts 3:19).
- Confess your sins and acknowledge Christ as your Lord (1 John 1:9; Romans 10:9).
- Forsake the sins you have confessed and repented of-the old lifestyle (Isaiah 55:7).
- Believe in Jesus Christ (John 3:16; Mark 16:16).
- Receive Jesus Christ (John 1:11-12; Revelation 3:20).

In a matter of moments, He did all of these! But our rejoicing was interrupted as the hospital staff came to take him to surgery.

In a few days, the old man was out of the hospital and his baby daughter took him to her home.

Me? In a few days, I moved to California.

Father, thank You is hardly enough to say to One who gave His Son for us. Words are insufficient, Lord Jesus, to express our gratefulness for the gift of Your innocent blood, shed for us. So we say only this: We are yours. Do with us as You will. Amen.

Chapter 12

PONDERING MARRIAGE

The two women-a mother and her daughter-walked into the Sunday morning worship service just as we were singing the opening hymn. They selected a pew and sat down. Both were well dressed and attractive.

They seemed uncomfortable as they nervously looked over the congregation. A helpful lady sitting behind them extended an open hymnal. The mother courteously accepted the book and held it in a way that her daughter could look on, but the daughter tried to ignore her. Not to be ignored, the mother nudged her daughter and then motioned for her to take one from the hymnal rack. Again, the daughter treated her mother like she was invisible. The mother's face flushed with anger and she pulled a hymnal from the rack and forced it upon her daughter.

From where I sat I could see that the anger in both

of them was about to burst, like an exploding volcano, through their Sunday faces (make-up and all). I really thought their next move would be out the front doors, but it wasn't. Both looked relieved when the music ended and they could return their hymnals to the rack.

At the close of the service, I stood at the door shaking hands. These new "friends" were in the line. The mother greeted me with compliments on the message and the friendliness of the people. She described the warmth and power she had felt in the service and how she was first drawn to the church when they passed by in a moving van on their way to their new home. She introduced me to her daughter. She also explained that her husband worked for the state and had to work some Sundays, but he would be attending church with them when he could.

I managed to get their names and address before they left, so I sent them a letter thanking them for attending and even stopped by to see them on Thursday. No one was at home. Neighbors said they had not been home all week.

Both mother and daughter returned the following Sunday. They thanked me for the letter I had sent and the card I left on the front door. They explained that they were still moving and had gone south for another load. However, they invited me back for a get-acquainted visit. We set the time for Thursday afternoon.

I kept the appointment, but only the daughter came to the door. She told me she was alone. I didn't go in, but told her I was returning to the office and asked her to have her parents call me when they came home. No call came.

During the next three months, the mother and daughter came to church only one time. I visited with the mother and daughter only once in their home and saw the husband/father once as he backed out of the garage and drove away. He saw me, too, waved, and continued driving. I rang the doorbell, but there was no answer. Later I phoned their home and a male voice answered. He said he was the daughter's boyfriend and they were just leaving.

That was my last attempt to contact them. In my heart, I knew they were not ready for a pastor and a church. I recalled other similar situations and concluded that, in time, perhaps they would be ready. I would wait.

Approximately 18 months later the phone rang. I answered and a voice charged with excitement shouted (nearly bursting my eardrum), "Hi, Pastor Yandell! Remember me?" I didn't, but soon discovered it was this mother.

"My daughter and her fiancé want to get married. They want to have the wedding in our church and they want our pastor to do the ceremony." She continued, "I am so excited . . . He is such a nice young man. They want to have the wedding right away. Is our church available, and would you do the ceremony around the 15th of next month?"

I waited for more from her before finally answering.

"Maybe," I said.

I asked if they already had the marriage license. They didn't.

Then I asked how old they were. He was 18. She was 16, but would soon be 17.

I suggested they check on getting their license, set a definite time for their wedding, and call me back. We would work on the wedding date when they had a definite time.

The mother called the next week. The couple had checked on getting their license and, just as I expected, they would have to have six hours of pre-marital counseling. She wanted to know if I was qualified to counsel them, or if they should see a credentialed marriage counselor.

I told her I had no counseling credentials, but I was an ordained minister, had talked with other couples and would talk with this couple if they wished me to.

"But there is this form for the counselor to sign," she said. I told her I was aware of the form and had signed several, which had always been accepted. I also informed her I would talk with the couple alone-she would not be allowed to sit in on any of the sessions.

There was silence. Then she muttered something about understanding, but she would have to bring them because neither the boy nor the girl had a car.

"I guess I could wait in the car while you talk with them," she said.

"That's a good guess," I replied.

Neither of us knew what to expect, but I was troubled about the whole thing. All I could do was just commit the days ahead to God and pray for wisdom. I wanted His will to be done. But would it?

I was awake at 3:00 a.m. My heavenly Father had awakened me on other occasions-always with a purpose. Sometimes, I awoke with a theme or series to preach or insight into a particular passage of Scripture I had been studying. On other occasions I awakened with a mental image of the name and face of individuals for whom I should pray.

In the darkness of this early morning a mother, a girl of 16, and a young man of 18 were on my mind. Why? My appointment with them was not for seven hours. I asked the One who awakened me what He had in mind. Prayer was the need.

I began to pray first for the mother who seemed too pushy-wanting her daughter married in a hurry. In fact, her insistence seemed more like the driving force in this whole process.

I prayed for the daughter, too. She seemed shy, had little to say, and seemingly no significant input into her own marriage plans.

Finally, I prayed for the confident young husband-to-be. He was a student. He was also self-assured and egotistical. He was fond of saying, "I can deal with that," but I confess that I was never really sure just what he meant.

The trio arrived at 10:00 a.m. When I heard their knock on the office door, I invited them to come in and stood to receive them. We exchanged greetings and the four of us remained standing. After a very long and awkward pause the mother announced that she would wait in the car. I told her this first session would be approximately 30 minutes.

As the door closed behind the exiting mother, I invited the young couple to have a seat. I stepped out from behind my desk and took a chair to the right of them, at a slight angle. In this arrangement we could have eye contact, but when questions or comments were uncomfortable we could easily look away without appearing to avoid each other or to end the conversation. (I've discovered it is very hard for some people, including me, to maintain a sustained eye contact.)

They seemed so tense that I decided to tell about a wedding I did where the bride got a little mixed up when repeating the marriage vows. She was to say, "I take you to be my lawful wedded husband. Instead, she said, "I take you to be my *awful* wedded husband." They laughed. It seemed to help us all relax a little.

I told the young couple I felt honored to be the one to do their counseling and wedding vows and the first thing I would ask of them was absolute honesty. They agreed. I could tell the girl was very sincere, a mark of maturity-even beyond her years. She would need that in the days that lay just ahead.

I began by giving each of them an opportunity to tell me, and each other, just what they would bring into the marriage in the way of family values and home managerial skills. (Such skills include things such as budgeting, balancing a checkbook, household chores, family planning, goal setting, sharing together, self-denial, etc.) Allowing for the time and place, I wasn't disappointed when neither of them could say anything more than just that they would love and take care of each other.

I reached for a file containing a pre-marital questionnaire I call, "Points to Ponder Before Marriage." I handed each of them a copy of the 36 questions I wanted them to study and answer in the privacy of their own homes. I instructed them that answers were to be written with absolute honesty and confidentiality. They were not to compare their answers until our next meeting. Neither were they to even consult or comment to each other about the questions. If they should have questions about the worksheets, they were to talk only to me. In our next session, we would begin reviewing their answers and working on any differences they may have. To this they agreed.

The three of us stood together and held hands. I prayed for God's blessings to rest upon them as they faced up to some hard questions and decisions that lay before them.

I thought of these "kids" several times during the weekend. As they came to mind, I would pray for them. I knew the assignment would be a challenge and could even change their wedding plans. Marriage is one of life's most important steps and this questionnaire reflected its seriousness.

Their assignment would first require them to define marriage according to their own individual understanding. This understanding would be influenced by their past exposure to marriage-in their own home and among their married relatives and friends. What they saw, or didn't see, in these marriages would cause them to list what they did and did not want in a marriage. They would need to know their own marriage was not to be a duplicate of their parents' marriage, nor any other. Instead, their marriage was to be different-having a uniqueness that the Lord builds into each marriage where He is allowed to work. Their feelings about divorce, remarriage, and the merging of two families would also be a subject of concern.

The questionnaire would ask each of them to define their particular role as husband or wife and to consider their eventual role as parents. Again, their understanding of these roles would also be influenced, to some degree, by their parents and other couples. I knew that some of these couples, although they have great influence on others, had no idea that they were role models. (The truth is that we're all role models to others, for good or bad.)

"Points to Ponder . . ." would also give them opportunity to express what they considered to be the most important ingredients of a good marriage. They would evaluate their ability to communicate, their friendship, and consider the things they enjoyed doing together. They would even be asked to name what the other one did that irritated them and what they didn't approve of in their spouse-to-be and hoped to change after the marriage. They would be forced-perhaps for the first time-to evaluate their habits and the way they handled both positive and negative emotions. These too play an important role in a successful marriage.

The management of their finances was another topic of importance. The questionnaire would lead them to detail their present financial obligations, earning power, and even divide the financial responsibilities both in and outside of their home.

They would also discuss their understanding of the importance of sex in marriage and their sexual expectations of each other. Past and present heath conditions, emotional stability, and the use of drugs and alcohol were another area of concern.

They would explain, as they saw it, the immediate and future adjustments each would have to make in the areas of culture, religion, and personal relationships. They would also have to explain whether they were willing to make these adjustments.

They would even have to consider how the church and Christianity would fit into their marriage and where they would go for help if they ever had a problem in marriage they couldn't seem to solve.

Finally, "Points to Ponder Before Marriage" would ask them to be honest with themselves and each other about why they wanted to get married and if they considered themselves ready for the responsibilities of marriage.

I prayed that God would guide them as they

considered these many factors that figured into the monumental decision they were about to make.

Monday passed. No phone call from the "kids." Suspecting that one, or both, of them were having second thoughts about getting married, I refrained from calling them.

Thursday, 9:00 a.m. The phone was ringing before I could unlock the office door. I answered with a smile in my usual way, "Good morning!" I heard weeping before I heard words. It was the mother of the bride-to-be.

"I don't need your service," she said. "My daughter isn't getting married-no thanks to you."

I asked for an explanation. She replied, "My daughter went through that paper you gave her and woke me up to say she wasn't getting married. She said it was more responsibility than she was ready to take on, and that it wasn't God's will for her to get married. And, besides, she wanted a marriage built on devotion-devotion to God and each other . . ."

Then the phone went dead. The next voice I heard said, "If you wish to make a call, please hang up and dial your number." The conversation was over, and I knew, so was our pastor/friend relationship.

I tried unsuccessfully to contact them over the next weekend. Their house was empty on Tuesday. In all the years since, I've not heard a word from any of them.

Father, thank You for all the tragedies and heartaches You have protected us from. Thank You for the mercy that sometimes foils our most ill-conceived plans. And thank You for the grace that forgives and restores when our ears are too dull to hear Your voice. Amen.

.

Chapter 13

TRAIN UP A CHILD

The windows of my office had thick cloudy panes that made it impossible to see more than just blurred objects outside. My work was interrupted by the sound of breaking glass. In my mind, I knew it was one of the windows of the auditorium. I peeked outside and confirmed my suspicions. Three young boys were throwing rocks and other objects at the windows.

Before confronting them, I called the police. I was told to try to detain them until help arrived. I looked at my watch. It was 4:00 p.m.

When I opened the door, two of the young boys ran. As I approached the one remaining boy he began spitting and cursing at me-daring me to touch him. He wanted a fight and I wanted to accommodate him. We were glaring at each other (I stayed just out of spitting range) when two detectives arrived. They heard him cursing me and daring me to touch him. They also saw him spitting at me.

(I've never understood how that kid had so much saliva when my mouth and throat were as dry as desert sand. I guess one of us was scared . . . and I think I know which one.)

The boy continued ranting until the detectives flashed their badges and identified themselves as police officers. One detective knew the boy from his past record. He was only nine years old when his behavior prompted a call to the police for the first time. Each time they had been called since then, his offense was more serious.

The boy's misdeeds were earning him some kind of rank in the gang to which he belonged. The frequency and seriousness of the crimes determined what position he held in the gang. This young boy was finding a warped sense of self-esteem in the gang and his crimes were growing more dangerous. Apparently, he found in the gang what he could not find at home.

The detectives said there wasn't much they could do and gave me the option of taking him home or having them do it. While they talked to the boy, I called three deacons who immediately came to the church.

The detectives agreed that we could meet with the boy and take him home when we were finished. Our meeting lasted until 6:30 p.m. The boy sulked, snarled, and threatened all through the meeting. He seemed unmoved by our reasoning and even the gospel.

It was after 7:00 p.m. when Cliff, one of the deacons, and I arrived at his house. I knocked on the door. His mother opened the door, and mistaking us for detectives, she screamed, "What kind of trouble are you in this time?" The boy stepped around her and went through the house and out the back door without saying a word. I quickly made introductions. She was relieved to know we were not detectives.

She began explaining how poor they were, that they could not pay for any damage, and how the boy was completely out of control. She said, "I don't know what happened. I've done all I can do, and I am about ready to give up on him."

The boy was 11 years of age.

We were never invited into the house, but from where I stood I could see a part of the dining area and living room. I could see a man, apparently sitting in his favorite chair, nursing a beer, and watching television. They were "pigging." The view I had told me what happened to their boy. The kid was just fleshing out the depraved nature with which he was born. Without the guidance he needed, he had been left to do as he wished and the result was predictable. I was thankful they had only one child.

For eight years I pastored near the slum area where this family lived. The area was called "The Flats." I knew that many godly people of several different denominations lived in this area. Their families were clean and their children were well behaved and respectful of their teachers and others in general. Their houses and yards were a reflection of the people who lived inside—people who loved God and one another. Though poor, these families were powerful examples of godly living.

The homes of these families reminded me of flowers blooming in a garbage dump. Their beauty and aroma surpassed the ugliness and stench that surrounded them. Their presence was a reminder that God can make a difference. He can, and does, grow flowers in the midst of refuse. These families were proof that God can make something beautiful out of any life. They prayed for their community and built churches to give hope and help to those who would respond.

The Flats continued to attract a large segment of people addicted to alcohol and other drugs. Low rent drew another segment of society to this area. These were people without order in their lives; families in which no one was in charge-where whoever was the loudest and strongest at the moment imposed their desires on the others.

Deacon Cliff and I were standing on the doorstep of just such a household. Could they be helped? Yes! Would they be helped? Probably not. Why? There was no evidence of a desire and will on their part to live differently. Without the desire and the will to do differently, there can be no change.

Orderly and godly living is not an accident. Nor does it come about without persistence and effort. There is no magic to change, but there is a miracle that will produce change for those who really want it. Jesus called it being born again (John 3:3). It is entrance into kingdom living and it results in flowers in the flats.

Cliff and I left. On our way to the church, he asked, "Pastor, what do you think happened that caused that boy to become a hoodlum by the time he was nine years old? Do you think there is any hope for him now?"

I looked at Cliff. He had a heart for people-especially doomed people. His eyes were filling with tears. His question was one I have been faced with many times before and since, occasioned by many situations. My answer has always gone something like this: "Actually, it was not only what happened to that boy to turn him into a criminal at such a tender age, it was also what did not happen. What happened is that this boy was left to follow the natural tendencies of his depraved nature."

In recent years, our nation has been repeatedly shocked when children commit heinous crimes against one another and even adults. Children, as young as 11 years of age, have been found guilty of murder. In one case, three boys—ages seven, eight, and 11—were charged with kidnapping, beating, and sexually assaulting a three-year-old girl. According to press reports, she was hit with a shoe and a brick, stripped of her clothing, and left in a water-filled concrete-lined creek.

When children commit such crimes they are tested and evaluated by psychologists and/or psychiatrists. These professionals try to determine what went so terribly wrong as to cause such young children to commit such hideous crimes. But will these specialists dare to consider spiritual causes for such behaviors? Some may. Most won't.

It will come as a shock to some, but every parent needs to know and believe their children are born and shaped in iniquity-conceived in sin-and are desperately wicked in their sinful nature (Psalm 51:5; Jeremiah 17:9; Romans 5:12). Theologians call this "total depravity" and it is the natural condition of every person who has lived since Adam and Eve (with the sole exception of Jesus Christ).

No child has to be taught or trained to do wrong. Their nature is to do wrong, and when left to rear themselves they will follow their depraved inclinations to whatever degree their bodies are capable-whether it is sexual sin, murder, stealing, or any of a number of other sinful behaviors.

In one sense, we are all "hoodlums" and criminals at birth. And, when the body grows sufficiently to carry out the tendencies of the sinful nature, we do. The Bible calls the sinful acts of young children "foolishness," not cuteness. Such foolishness is bound in the heart of every child and only the "rod of correction" will drive it out (Proverbs 22:15). That's *loving* correction, not cruelty.

In one sense, the parent is the child's first "god," and the way the child relates to his or her parent will in some degree influence the way they will relate to the true God as they move through the various ages and maturity levels. When parents teach their children to obey, respect, and honor them, they are also teaching them the first lesson of obeying, respecting, and honoring God.

Our family still enjoys a good laugh when recalling what one of our grandsons said. He asked a babysitter, "What is God's last name?" "I don't know," she replied. "What do you think it is?" He gave it some thought, and as he walked away he was heard to say, "Probably Yandell." He was wrong, of course, but his answer still reminds us all that children look to their parents in developing their concept of God.

Why did this boy in Oklahoma City end up a hardened criminal before he was even a teenager? Nobody cared enough to demonstrate the love of God in His life—the love that says no as well as yes.

Is there any hope for such children? The answer to that question is always yes, providing the child receives the kind of help he needs—the kind that deals with the inner person; the kind of help that leads him to the God who can change His heart.

Father, the seeds of rebellion have been sown in our hearts from our earliest days. Whenever they sprout—however small they may be—You have our permission to pull them up by the roots. Amen.

Chapter 14

WHATEVER HAPPENED TO TROY?

The first mention of Troy that I heard came from a relative of mine. She said he was a likeable boy around 10 or 11 years of age. "He's really a good boy that does bad things," she added.

This relative had worked with Troy's mother at one time and suggested that she and Troy attend our church since we had a "bus" ministry (a van, actually) and could give them transportation. She gave me their phone number and asked me to give them a call since they had expressed an interest in coming to Sunday School and worship.

I called the number the next day around 4:00 p.m. My call was well received and I made an appointment to see them on Saturday at 10:00 a.m. I prayed for them until Saturday and went prepared to enroll them in Sunday School.

When I arrived at their house I noticed a badly neglected yard and an old car parked in the driveway. I could tell the car had not been moved for a long time. The right rear tire was flat, and there was a large puddle of oil under the motor.

As I walked toward the house I noticed a broken pane in the front window with a large weather-beaten pillow stuffed in the hole. Needless to say, my first impression of the place was that it was neglected and run down.

My thoughts went to the people inside, Troy and his mom. I could not keep from wondering if these two precious people I was about to meet were as badly neglected as the place where they lived. If so, it would take a lot of time and effort on our part while God brought renewal and restoration to this family. I continued my slow walk toward the house; curious about the visit I was about to experience.

I knocked on the door and waited for a response. No answer came. I could hear a television playing loudly inside. I knocked again, only louder, so it could be heard above the noise of the TV.

This time my knocking worked. Troy came to the door—still in his PJ's. His auburn hair stood up on the back of his head. But, in the front it was drooping down over his forehead to his eyebrows. He was cradling a bowl of cold cereal in his left arm while his right hand was busy selecting just the right amount for another bite.

When he lifted his head to look at me I noticed a sprinkling of freckles across his high cheekbones and nose. While there was no twinkle in his eyes, or a smile on his lips, I liked Troy immediately and was eager to make friends with him.

I introduced myself and requested to speak with his mother. Very politely, Troy responded, "Wait just a minute, please." He turned to walk away but hesitated, as though he was puzzled about what to do about the door. "Excuse me," he said, and closed the door. I was impressed with this little guy's manners.

On the porch, I waited and listened. I thought I heard footsteps and muffled talking inside. Soon the door swung open and Troy's mother stood there peering through the screen. We were meeting for the first time and she appeared to be a little embarrassed. She stood about five-and-a-half feet tall and was clothed in a floor-length robe. She brushed a lock of blonde, definitely-slept-in, hair out of her eyes and tried to focus on me. Her sleepy eyes said she had been awakened from a sound sleep. Her face was pale and still showing signs of yesterday's makeup.

When I introduced myself, her expression changed to one of shock and she began apologizing. She had forgotten our appointment, but was quick to assure me that Troy would be coming to Sunday School and worship tomorrow. She wanted to know when he should be ready and promised he would go. I told her I would pick Troy up first, around 9:00 a.m.

By then, Troy had returned to his TV program and seemed totally oblivious to what was happening at the door. I didn't pre-enroll him in Sunday School as I had planned, nor did I put his name on the riders list. I had my doubts about the success of my screen door visit.

Sunday, 9:00 a.m. I stopped the bus in front of Troy's house. To my surprise, before I could even honk the horn, he burst through the door, running at full speed toward the bus. As he climbed in I greeted him and asked how it was going for him. He replied, "I'm in trouble." I would hear those words from him frequently in the days to come.

Troy took a seat at the front of the bus. This made it convenient for me to introduce him to the other riders as they got on. At first, Troy would just say hi and look at the floor. But on about the third stop he saw someone he knew—they had gone to the same school before Troy had to move. By the time we arrived at the church Troy was opening up and talking with the other riders. I thought it was a good sign.

I took Troy home last that afternoon because I wanted to talk with him. It would be the first of many times when Troy and I had a few minutes to just talk alone. He told me he enjoyed Sunday School and the youth church worship time. When he talked about his family, however, that was a different story.

His dad had moved out when Troy was in the first grade. There were no parting words for him. He came home from school and his dad was gone. He never heard from him and did not know where he was.

Troy's mother was a hard-working single mom trying to care for herself and her son. She was a waitress at a local restaurant, but sometimes had to work two jobs. When her car broke down she walked or a friend gave her a ride.

When I inquired about his alone time at home, Troy said he was never alone. There was always an adult with him. Sometimes it was a grandparent, who lived about ten miles away. Other times, it was a neighbor or his mom's friend.

This is how my ministry with Troy began. In one sense, I didn't have much to go on. But in another sense, I had a lot to go on. I had to be careful about forming early opinions and jumping to conclusions. I realized I couldn't take his dad's place, but I could love him, and perhaps do some things a caring father would do for his son.

Troy became a regular bus rider for Sunday School and morning worship. He always came running toward the bus, but not as an act of enthusiasm for church. It was more like an act of obedience to a harsh command or threat. (I never knew for sure just what propelled him.) I was impressed with Troy's clean clothes, combed hair, and shined shoes. In my heart, I believed someone was behind his neat appearance. I just didn't think a little boy would always be that neat if he dressed himself.

While Troy's appearance was always commendable, I could not say the same about his attitude. Almost every Sunday he seemed angry—lashing out at the other children or sulking. His behavior was, at the least, unpredictable.

One Sunday, on the way to church, Troy and Christine—who was about the same age—got into an argument on the bus. She tried hard to think of appropriate words to express herself. Finally, she shouted, "TROY! TROY! TROY! You are just . . . you are just . . . you are just a TROY!"

As I pulled the bus to a stop at the curb everyone became quiet. Christine looked me straight in the eye and said, "Pastor, I'm sorry." I turned to face Troy, who was sitting directly behind me. He fixed his eyes on the floor and without looking up said, "I'm sorry for my part." I was impressed with their apparent sincerity. I accepted their apologies and continued our trip to church. Before unloading, I thanked the children for a good ride. On the way to class I made plans to talk with Troy when I took him home. A talk with Christine would come later.

On the return trip, I was looking forward to a little

talk with Troy. I knew it would be brief, but it would be a start. I prayed silently for the right words and for wisdom. Neither Troy nor I spoke during the last few miles to his house. When we arrived, I parked the bus just short of their driveway.

Troy sensed I wanted to talk to him. He clearly thought I was about to scold him so he gazed out the bus window and emotionally braced himself for a volley of unkind words—the kind he'd heard many times before.

My young friend looked puzzled and surprised when I told him I was proud of him and Christine for the respect they had shown to me and for their sincere apology. Without referring to his problems and periodic anger I told Troy he was special to God because God had created him for a purpose and God had a really great plan for his life. I also talked with him about discovering that plan for his life by learning to talk with God about everything and everybody—including himself, his problems, and especially his feelings of anger.

I also confessed to Troy that I had my own problem with anger when I was about his age and how my anger lasted all through my growing-up years and even into young adulthood. Troy relaxed and wanted to hear more. I had opened myself up to him and was now vulnerable and I had piqued his curiosity. I silently prayed, asking God how much I should share with a little boy who seemed to be starting down a road I had once traveled.

Time was passing and I needed to give some thought as to how much from my own experiences I should share with Troy. I also knew there would be an adult inside the house waiting for Troy to come home from church. Just then the front door to Troy's home opened and a woman I had not met came walking briskly toward the bus. I asked Troy about her and he identified her as his mother's friend who was to take care of him until his mother came home from work. I knew my silent prayer had been answered. I would have the time I needed to think through just how much I should share from my own personal experiences.

Troy picked up his things to leave. I told him I had enjoyed talking with him and asked if we might talk some more next Sunday. He said, "Yaaah, dude, I would like that." I met his mother's friend and explained that I needed to get acquainted with Troy. They seemed comfortable with each other and waved to me as I drove away.

The following Sunday, Troy and I talked again. I told him about my anger as a little boy and how older people in my life would threaten me with punishment if I didn't straighten up. I also spoke of my response to these situations. I would cooperate with the old people's demands to sit down, shut up, apologize, or whatever, until they were satisfied. Then I would go off to myself to stomp around, hit things, throw things, and sulk. In my sulking, I would talk to myself about what I would do when I got bigger.

I ventured to tell Troy more. I decided to fast forward to when I got bigger. My anger got worse. My temper tantrums also worsened, although they were not recognizable to some people because I controlled myself around certain people. But inside of me, I felt as though I was going to explode. As some would say, I felt like I was losing it—and at times, I did.

I could see Troy was having difficulty mentally processing what I had said. While our experiences and responses were similar, Troy didn't appear to see an application to his present situation. He had questions that needed answers, but before I could work on answers I would need to draw the questions out of him.

Troy and I began looking forward to our one-on-one minutes together each Sunday. During those times we talked about various things, including his family and how he felt toward his dad and mom. We discussed how he felt inside himself and his feelings about his friends. We even talked about what he wanted to be and do when he became an adult.

One particular Sunday, I thought I would probe and ask him to tell me about his dad. "He didn't like me," was his response. He continued, "My dad left me and Mom when I was in first grade. That's all I know." He then became quiet with his head bowed and his eyes fixed on the bus floor.

I waited momentarily before asking, "Is that all you know, or is it that you just don't want to talk about it?"

"I don't want to talk about it," he said with a touch of anger in his voice. He raised his head and I could see tears in his eyes.

I backed off from questioning him. I didn't need for him to dwell on his painful past. It would just add fuel to the glowing embers of anger that lay smoldering in the ashes of yesterday. Why stir up a past he could do nothing about?

Rick Warren says there are three basic causes of anger:

- Pain—when someone, or something, has hurt you.
- Frustration—when you are in a situation you do not understand and cannot do anything about.

- Insecurity—when you feel unloved, unwanted, or uncertain about the future.

When someone hurts us, we get angry. When we are frustrated, we get angry. When we are insecure, we get angry.

Troy had all three of these basic reasons for being angry. He was suffering perpetual pain from an emotional wound inflicted on him when his dad left and his family fell apart. After five or six years the injury to his feelings and emotions was still open and oozing poison into his spiritual and emotional system. Things he could not understand frustrated him, and the situation he was in deprived him of the relationships and achievements enjoyed by his peers. He was insecure—unable to feel safe, cared for, or protected. This uneasiness made him uncomfortable and fearful.

Out of his pain, frustration, and insecurity came the expressions of his anger—lashing out at others to hurt them, sulking, and being unpredictable, kept him in trouble with those who were trying to help him.

I recall one Sunday when Troy got on the bus and I greeted him.

"How's it goin'?" I asked.

"I'm in trouble," he answered,

"Now what did you do to get in trouble?" I inquired.

"I just got up!"

I could not restrain myself from laughing at his reply. But to him it was no laughing matter. Every day started and ended with him being in trouble. I saw humor in Troy's answer but I also saw a little boy who was deeply troubled.

I felt a little nudge (from the Holy Spirit, no doubt)

to talk with him at that moment. I checked the mirrors to see if there were any cars behind me. There weren't, so I pulled the van to the side of the street and parked.

Troy was surprised that I stopped. "Am I in trouble?" he asked.

"No, Troy, you are not in trouble," I responded. "I just want to talk with you for a few minutes." I checked my watch. I could use five minutes and still be at church on time for Sunday School.

I used my five minutes reviewing Troy's situation, as I understood it. I did not belittle his parents, nor excuse them for their behavior. I simply emphasized that his parents were responsible for their own choices, decisions, and actions. I tried to help Troy understand that what happened between them and the break-up of their home was not his fault. I urged him not to blame himself for something he did not do.

My five minutes went fast and soon it was time to finish the route. But before continuing on, I prayed for Troy and his family.

After the morning worship service I was loading the bus for the ride home. Troy was missing. I sounded the horn for the riders to come. Mike, our youth pastor, brought Troy to the bus. Like so many others had done in his past, I thought Troy was in trouble. Instead, Mike asked Troy to tell me something. He was a little shy, but said that he had invited Jesus into his heart in the youth church service! We rejoiced together.

When I arrived at his house we began our one-on-one moments together. I tried to encourage him in his step of faith and told him Jesus would help him with his anger. We talked about Bible studies and baptism. I asked if he could tell his mom and others who helped care for him how he had invited Jesus into his heart. He said he could and would.

I had great expectations of working with Troy, and his mom, concerning his spiritual growth. I learned later that Mike was also excited and looking forward to helping Troy learn to follow Jesus. Everything was go!

I watched Troy as he exited the bus, making his way toward his front door. There seemed to be a different walk about him. I thanked God and gave Him praise for Troy...not knowing this would be my last time to see him.

The following Sunday I went to pick up Troy. When I pulled up to the house I had a sinking feeling. There were no signs of life around the house. The grass was tall. The old car was still in the driveway and the weather-worn pillow was still stuffed in the broken window pane. The front door was ajar. I looked inside to see only litter. They had moved. I never knew when or where. Nor have I ever ceased to wonder whatever happened to Troy.

Father, the world is full of Troys—hurting kids, victims of the actions of others. They drop into our lives and then out again. But they never disappear from Your sight or slip off the edges of Your "radar." We look forward to the day when we will see them again and rejoice in the work You have done in and through their lives. Amen.

Chapter 15

WHATEVER HAPPENED TO CHRISTINE?

I first met Christine at a wedding rehearsal. I had accepted an invitation to do a wedding ceremony with a western flair. No horses and saddles, just jeans, boots, large hats, and tuxedo coats. I had none of this garb on hand and had no plans to buy them just for the wedding. I had requested permission to wear my black "marryin'-and-buryin'" suit instead. The couple agreed.

The rehearsal was to be held at a small ranch north of Visalia, California, the city where I lived. The rancher was in the process of building a barn. There would be a hayloft, feeding troughs, storage space for sacks of feed, and shop space. The wedding would be held in the shop space.

The rehearsal was late getting started. The people were getting uncomfortable and restless. Some had begun drinking beer from cans and stronger stuff from bottles obscured by paper bags.

I noticed a small girl, about seven years of age, who seemed lost in the crowd of adults and teens. She was trying very hard to have a conversation with someone, without much success. She went from one huddle of people to the next, hoping to be received into the group. She wasn't fitting in. I knew how she must have felt—I wasn't fitting in either.

She finally came toward me as her last resort. She was obviously uneasy and shy, as though she was testing me for a response. Would at least the minister talk with her? Or would she remain alone and lonely in the crowd?

"Hi," she said softly.

I greeted her enthusiastically, commenting about her being the youngest person at the wedding and how glad I was that she came over to say hello. Thus began our conversation and our friendship. Art Linkletter used to say, "Kids say the darnedest things." I was about to find out just how right he was about children.

In a matter of moments I found out a lot about the little girl. Her name was Christine and the young man getting married was her cousin. She was going to be the flower girl for the wedding and would wear a white cowgirl dress, complete with a white hat and boots. And that's not all. Her grandma lived in Missouri and she would be at the wedding, and she was a Christian. (I would learn the significance of this statement much later.)

Someone called out that they were ready to begin

the rehearsal. Christine and I walked together to where the wedding party had gathered at the rear of the barn around bales of hay. It would be my job to walk the wedding party through the rehearsal a couple of times. With all the clownishness going on, I could only hope the actual wedding would be better. If it weren't, the whole affair would be in total disarray.

On Saturday, the actual wedding began right on time with me positioned at the west end of the barn between bales of hay. Looking up, I saw Christine coming toward me. She was dazzling in her white cowgirl dress—complete with white hat and boots—and she carried a small basket of white flowers. She outshined the entire wedding party.

The wedding went well and it was followed by a reception. It was at the reception that Christine brought her mother to meet me.

"Pastor, this is my mom," she said. I never even got her name and, though I would make repeated efforts over the next five years, it would be the only time I would see her. Her mother turned and started walking away. Christine, still holding her mother's hand, looked back over her shoulder and called out, "I want to go to your church."

"Where do you live?" I called back.

"At the College Inn, for now," was her answer. "I'll call you."

They were gone with relatives.

I knew very little about the College Inn. I was told there was a lot of drug traffic there and the low rent—by the day, week, or month—made it a very popular place for college students and low-income individuals. I could not imagine a mother making such a place "home" for herself and her little girl. I doubted I would ever hear from them again. I was wrong.

It was 10:00 p.m. on Saturday when Christine called to ask what time the bus would pick her up for Sunday School and worship. (The small church pastor does a little of everything and at that time I drove the church van/bus.) I set the time for 9:15 a.m. and wondered about a seven-year-old girl calling at that time of night for a ride to church. Where was her mother? Did her mother know she made the call? Why wasn't this little girl in bed asleep? Should I take the call seriously or just forget the whole matter? Even if I had wanted to, I *couldn't* forget.

Sunday, 9:15 a.m. As I drove toward the College Inn office I first saw a lighted "vacancy" sign, then I saw Christine standing near the front office door. She was dressed in her white cowgirl dress—the one she wore to the wedding on Saturday afternoon. (She would wear the same dress every Sunday for the next several months.)

Christine boarded the bus full of excitement and eager for Sunday School and worship. She wanted to know how far it was to church, when we would get there, who her teacher would be, and a half-dozen other things. It was the beginning of a growing love for church.

As time passed and Christine and I became better acquainted she began telling me her incredible story. She spoke often of her mother's addiction to drugs and her endless line of live-in boyfriends. She also told me of her brother, three years older than her, who lived in Missouri with their grandmother. She said her mother moved frequently, but she did not know why. Christine assured me, however, that she would always let me know where to pick her up for church. She loved her church!

The more I knew, the more concerned I became for Christine. I often questioned in my own mind if I should report this situation to the authorities. Yet, although I feared for Christine, I could not feel certain about reporting the situation to anyone. Instead, my means of getting help for her would be prayer. I committed Christine to God and earnestly prayed for Him to protect her from harm and provide for her needs. I didn't know how God would answer my prayers, but I was confident He would. He did!

Christine missed a Sunday. Her mother had moved again and Christine had no way of calling me. On Tuesday, she called me with the new address and asked for a ride on Wednesday night. I gave her a time when I would pick her up on the van/bus.

Christine was ready when I arrived, but she appeared depressed and, for the first time, she looked shabby. I felt bad for her.

This move was the proverbial "straw that broke the camel's back." Christine did not like her mother's new live-in boyfriend. She complained that he watched her every move and did not want her to go anyplace, not even church. He insisted that she call him "Dad," but she refused. He constantly talked about her growing into womanhood and what a beautiful woman she was going to be. Understandably, Christine became extremely uncomfortable and afraid to go to bed at night. The sight of him in the morning repulsed her.

"Pastor, what can I do?" she asked as I drove toward the church.

As I continued to drive, I prayed silently for words to use in answering her question. I recalled the times I had prayed for her and my concern and fears for her. I also remembered that I had committed her to God and was continuing to trust Him to watch over her and protect her from harm. Was I about to become part of the answer to my prayers?

Time had passed quickly. It had been five years since I first met Christine at her cousin's wedding. She was now 12 years old and would be 13 before school started. Christine got on the van/bus one Sunday with obvious mixed emotions. I knew something was troubling her and I feared the worst. She told me it would be her last Sunday. She was moving back east to live with her grandmother. She would be traveling by bus; leaving on Tuesday at 2:30 p.m. Christine explained that she had called Child Protective Services on her own. A worker came out and met with her mother. Phone calls were made back east to the grandmother. Everything was quickly arranged.

Christine said goodbye that Sunday and left the bus crying. She looked back once and I waved to her. She returned the wave, and the door closed behind her. I drove away with a heavy heart, but confident that God was answering my prayers.

On Tuesday, I drove unannounced to the bus station, hoping to see Christine one more time before she boarded the big bus to Grandma's. As I entered the bus station I saw Christine and the social worker sitting together. Three bulging grocery sacks sat between them. There was no luggage or boxes, only the sacks containing everything Christine had, and some fruit the social worker had bought for her to eat on the trip. She had no other food or money and only the social worker and me to see her off.

We had a few minutes before departure time. I gave Christine some money for the trip. We prayed together and talked about her new start in life. I told her she could call my wife, Winnie, and me collect just as soon as she got to her grandmother's home. I also told her she could call us collect once a month and talk as long as she liked. At first she said no, until I told her we did that for other young people whose lives we had been involved in. She thanked me. During our conversation I could sense God at work—watching over her and protecting her from harm.

Christine's first call came when she arrived at Grandma's. She said it had been a 30-hour trip and she ate all of the fruit and bought some food with her money when the bus made a rest stop. Her grandma had already made plans to take her and her brother shopping for school clothes. (That's what grandmas do, don't you know?)

The second call came just a month later. Christine was excited. She was signed up for school and would be attending the same one as her older brother.

The third call came just a month later. Christine was still excited and enjoying the new school. She had made some new friends and found a church that reminded her of our church in California. (Isn't God good?)

As Christine settled into school and church her calls became less frequent. Sometime after the first of the year, she called while Winnie was at work. She was heartbroken. She wanted prayer for her brother who had become involved in drugs at school. He was in deep trouble.

Christine called a few more times, but her calls were getting further apart. In time, we were left wondering, whatever happened to Christine?

Finally, after several years, Christine called again. She was calling from Atlanta, Georgia. She had finished high school, attended a trade school, and was now employed by the state of Georgia. And, oh, the BIG news—she had met the love of her life! After two years of dating, her dream man was now her fiancée. He, too, was employed by the state of Georgia and Christine was eagerly looking forward to marriage and a family. We, of course, wished for them many years of happiness!

Our Father in Heaven, thank You for watching over all the Christines of this world against whom the odds are highly stacked. Thank You for allowing people like us to share Your love with them and be a part of the answer to our prayers. Amen.

.